Cincinnati Reds IQ: The Ultimate Test of True Fandom

Tucker Elliot
& Joe Soriano

2011 Edition
(Volume I)

Printed in the United States of America.
Copyright © 2011 by Tucker Elliot & Joe Soriano.

This title is part of the IQ sports trivia book series, which is a trademark of Black Mesa Publishing, LLC.

Cataloging-in-Publication Data is available from the Library of Congress.

ISBN: 978-0-9837922-4-6
First edition, first printing.

Cover photo courtesy of Mark Whitt.
Cover design by Holly Walden Ross.

Black Mesa Publishing, LLC
Florida
David Horne and Marc CB Maxwell
Black.Mesa.Publishing@gmail.com

www.blackmesabooks.com

Cincinnati Reds IQ

Contents

Introduction   1

Sparky Anderson   5

Joe Morgan   15

Johnny Bench   27

Pete Rose   37

George Foster   49

Tony Pérez   61

Dave Concepción   73

Ken Griffey   85

César Gerónimo   97

Gary Nolan   105

About the Authors   115

References   116

About Black Mesa   117

"The Big Red Machine teams will never be forgotten ... They'll be remembered because of the professionals they had, the character they had, the skill they had. Those teams were a symbol of what baseball really should be."
— Johnny Bench

Introduction

I HAVE A Cincinnati Reds 1978 Yearbook Magazine that my dad paid $1.50 for at a Spring Training game in Tampa, FL. Pete Rose is on the cover with the caption "Pete Rose and the 3,000 Hit Club" and inside the magazine is an article on his quest to reach 3,000 hits (he began the season needing just 34 to become only the 13th player in history to reach that plateau). It also discusses his goal to become the National League's all-time hits leader ... no mention of the MLB record Rose would later eclipse.

On page 7 is a great picture of Tom Seaver—and lucky for me, mine is autographed. Same with the picture of Paul Moskau on page 13, George Foster on page 17, and Davey Concepción on page 25.

It's a great souvenir that brings back a lot of memories—and thanks to Spring Training, Cincinnati was my "first" team.

Later, my first regular season major league game was Atlanta vs. Cincinnati and my favorite player, Johnny Bench, hit a grand slam.

After writing or collaborating on more than two dozen baseball history and trivia books, I'm glad I finally have the opportunity to write about and pay tribute to one of baseball's great franchises, and the one that helped instill my lifelong love for the game when I was just a kid.

Sparky Anderson wasn't just my favorite manager ... he was my *mom's* favorite manager.

And in our backyard wiffle ball games, my brothers and I stood at the plate and imitated the batting stances of Pete Rose, Joe Morgan, George Foster, Tony Pérez, and Johnny Bench.

We even practiced flapping our back elbows like Joe Morgan as we tried to imagine what it was like to be a two-time MVP, a World Series hero, and a two-time World Champion ... in back-to-back seasons.

We worked hard to be like the guys on the mound, too. Our favorite was Tom Seaver, of course. If you didn't hit dirt with your right knee when you shoved off the mound, well ... then you just didn't have what it took to be like Tom Terrific.

Later it was Mario Soto, and later still it was Jose Rijo ... but no matter what the year, the team was always the Cincinnati Reds. I hope this book brings back many great baseball memories for you, just as it did for me.

This is a book of history and trivia that covers all eras of Reds baseball—however, to honor the legacy of Sparky Anderson and the Big Red Machine, we have chosen to introduce each chapter of questions with a profile of one of the players from that extraordinary era ... but we'll begin with the man who led them: Sparky Anderson.

Now sit back, challenge yourself, and enjoy.

Tucker Elliot
Tampa, FL
August 2011

.

"I got good players, stayed out of their way, let them win a lot, and then just hung around for 26 years."
— Sparky Anderson, Hall of Fame Induction Speech

Sparky Anderson

WHEN SPARKY ANDERSON began his tenure as Reds manager in 1970 his resume had a few glaring holes. Historically, success as a player at the big league level does not necessarily translate to success as a big league manager—in fact, the opposite is more often true. In the fall of 1969 and continuing through spring of 1970, however, Sparky Anderson's playing career (or lack thereof) was the opening argument diehard fans used when speaking out against the newly hired skipper.

It was an easy target, considering his big league career consisted of one year playing second base for the Phillies.

In 1959, Sparky batted just .218 in 152 games. Only 12 of his 104 big league hits went for extra bases ... and none of them left the yard. He was your typical scrappy middle infielder, slight in build but heavy in what he called "spit and vinegar." Sparky was relegated to Triple-A ball in 1960, again in 1961, again in 1962, and yet again in 1963.

In 1964, the 30-year-old ballplayer hung up his spikes after 11 professional seasons and decided to earn a living painting houses.

That argument alone was enough for many to rest the case against Sparky—but for others there was a much stronger and entirely valid point to be made against his hiring, and it was simply this: he'd never managed a big league team before. When General Manager Bob Howsam announced on October 9, 1969, that Sparky Anderson would take over as Reds skipper for 1970, papers all across Ohio ran this headline the following day: "Sparky Who?" Cincinnati had loads of talent ... but was it realistic to expect a rookie manager to lead the franchise?

Howsam thought so—in fact, he said of Sparky, "We had some very good players but they needed to know how to do certain things. We thought they needed work in fundamentals and Sparky was extremely capable of that."

Sparky's rise to the rank of big league manager had gone much quicker than his path to becoming a big league player—and his career as a manager would last 25 years longer and be infinitely more successful. After paying his dues as a minor league skipper from 1964 through 1968, Sparky joined the San Diego Padres coaching staff in 1969. And with one season as a major league coach under his belt, in 1970 he began his journey to the Hall of Fame as the manager of the Cincinnati Reds.

It took exactly one month of regular season play for fans to accept Sparky—posting a 16-6 record out of the gate has that kind of effect. The club won 20 more games in May, and by the time July 26 rolled around, Cincinnati beat St. Louis 12-5 in the season's 100th game as the Reds improved to 70-30 and increased their Division lead to 12.5 games.

The Reds were a more human 32-30 the rest of the way, but that was more than good enough to clinch a Division title by 14.5 games over the Los Angeles Dodgers. Sparky then led the Reds to a clean sweep of the Pittsburgh Pirates to claim the National League Pennant—and despite falling in five games to the Baltimore Orioles during the 1970 World Series, it was clear to anyone paying attention that Cincinnati was on the verge of something special.

His tenure with the club would last nine seasons and 1,450 regular season games and result in 863 wins—Bill McKechnie is the only other skipper to manage the Reds for as many seasons as Sparky, but no one has been at the helm for more games or wins.

There was, of course, a sophomore slump in 1971 that saw the Reds finish a disappointing fifth in the standings.

However, Cincinnati then reeled off four Division titles in five seasons—including back-to-back World Series titles in 1975 and 1976 that cemented the legacy of Sparky Anderson and The Big Red Machine. And for Sparky, who was elected to the Baseball Hall of Fame by the Veterans Committee in 2000, it is his legacy as the manager of the Big Red Machine that endures and has earned him a place among the game's truly elite skippers. Very few who manage a big league club are successful, fewer still are the ones who experience success over an extended period of time, but to achieve a level of success so extraordinary that it is given a category all it's own—"The Big Red Machine"—places Sparky in one of the most exclusive and elite clubs in baseball history.

TOP OF THE FIRST

QUESTION 1: He managed the club for nine seasons and seven times won 90-plus games. He was also the manager of the Big Red Machine. Who is this legend and what is the number retired in his honor?

QUESTION 2: He was an All-Star shortstop who became the team captain in 1983. Who is this legend and what is the number retired in his honor?

QUESTION 3: Major League Baseball honors this former manager annually when an award that bears his name is given to a current ballplayer "who best exemplifies [his] character and fighting spirit." Who is this legend and what is the number retired in his honor? His number was the first in franchise history to be retired.

QUESTION 4: He was a ten-time All-Star, five-time Gold Glover, two-time league MVP, and two-time World Champion with the Big Red Machine. Who is this legend and what is the number retired in his honor?

QUESTION 5: Cincinnati's official website calls him "perhaps the greatest catcher to ever play in the major leagues." Who is this legend and what is the number retired in his honor?

QUESTION 6: The Reds' official website calls him "the heart and soul of Cincinnati's Big Red Machine." He was the third member of the Big Red Machine to be inducted into the Baseball Hall of Fame when he was enshrined on July 23, 2000. Who is this legend and what is the number retired in his honor?

QUESTION 7: He blasted 30-plus homers seven times during ten seasons (1956-65) with Cincinnati to begin his Hall of Fame career. Who is this legend and what is the number retired in his honor?

QUESTION 8: Cincinnati's official website says "he was noted as the greatest left handed slugger and one of the best fielding first basemen in club history." He hit 251 homers for the Reds from 1947-57. Who is this legend and what is the number retired in his honor?

QUESTION 9: This baseball icon is the only player to have his number retired by every major league team—including Cincinnati, although he never played for the Reds. Who is this legend and what is the number retired in his honor?

QUESTION 10: He's arguably the greatest baseball player not yet in the Hall of Fame—and so far (as of 2011) he's not even in the Cincinnati Reds Hall of Fame, but he's still a legend. Who is this legendary pariah and what jersey number did he wear for Cincinnati?

TOP OF THE FIRST ANSWER KEY

___ **QUESTION 1:** Sparky Anderson, #10
___ **QUESTION 2:** Dave Concepción, #13
___ **QUESTION 3:** Fred Hutchinson, #1
___ **QUESTION 4:** Joe Morgan, #8
___ **QUESTION 5:** Johnny Bench, #5
___ **QUESTION 6:** Tony Pérez, #24
___ **QUESTION 7:** Frank Robinson, #20
___ **QUESTION 8:** Ted Kluszewski, #18
___ **QUESTION 9:** Jackie Robinson, #42
___ **QUESTION 10:** Pete Rose, #14

KEEP A RUNNING TALLY OF YOUR CORRECT ANSWERS!

Number correct: ___ / 10

Overall correct: ___ / 10

BOTTOM OF THE FIRST

QUESTION 11: Harry Dalton, a legendary baseball executive in his own right, said of this Reds legend, "Every time [he] throws, everybody in baseball drools." Who is the legend Dalton was referring to?

QUESTION 12: He spent six years playing second base for Cincinnati but he's in the Hall of Fame because of his managerial career in the Bronx. It was in New York where he won three World Championships, the first three in Yankees franchise history. Can you name the second baseman that became a managerial legend in the Bronx?

QUESTION 13: Fellow-Hall of Famer Billy Herman said of this Reds legend, "If he were playing today, on this artificial surface, I don't know where the infielders would play him. The ball comes off there like a rocket, and the way [he] hit it, he might kill an infielder today. He could hit a ball as hard as anybody I ever saw, and that includes Ruth and Foxx." Can you name the Hall of Fame catcher Herman was referring to?

QUESTION 14: In his Hall of Fame induction speech, this legend said, "I take my vote as a salute to the little guy, the one who doesn't hit 500 home runs. I was one of the guys that did all they could to win." Do you know which legend spoke those words?

QUESTION 15: This slugger once said, "Pitchers did me a favor when they knocked me down. It made me more determined. I wouldn't let that pitcher get me out. They say you can't hit if you're on your back, but I didn't hit on my back. I got up." And trust me, pitchers feared this legendary slugger. Can you name him?

QUESTION 16: Reggie Jackson once said of this pitching legend, "He's so good that blind people come to the park just to hear him pitch." Not exactly sure how tactful that statement was, but he really did say it. Who was Jackson referring to?

QUESTION 17: In Game 7 of the 1975 World Series, the Boston Red Sox led Cincinnati 3-0 during the sixth inning when this player hit a two-run homer to jumpstart the Reds offense. Bill Lee, who was pitching for Boston, said, "I had been having good success with [him], throwing him my slow, arching curveball, so I thought it would be a good idea to throw it to him again. Unfortunately, so did [he], who timed it beautifully. He counted the seams of the ball as it floated up to the plate, checked to see if Lee MacPhail's signature was on it, signed his own name to it, and then jumped all over it." Who homered against Lee to spark the Reds comeback vs. the Red Sox?

QUESTION 18: On August 26, 1939, Cincinnati met the Brooklyn Dodgers in the first game to be televised on live TV. The Dodgers won the game 6-1, but this Reds third baseman became the first player in baseball history to bat on live TV. Do you know his name?

QUESTION 19: He won his first career batting title with a .335 average in 1968. With that title, he also became the first switch-hitter in N.L. history to win a batting crown. Who is this switch-hitter?

QUESTION 20: This legendary Reds manager became the first skipper in baseball history to manage and lose the All-Star Game for both the National League and the American League. Can you name him?

BOTTOM OF THE FIRST ANSWER KEY

___ **QUESTION 11:** Johnny Bench
___ **QUESTION 12:** Miller Huggins
___ **QUESTION 13:** Ernie Lombardi
___ **QUESTION 14:** Joe Morgan
___ **QUESTION 15:** Frank Robinson
___ **QUESTION 16:** Tom Seaver
___ **QUESTION 17:** Tony Pérez
___ **QUESTION 18:** Billy Werber
___ **QUESTION 19:** Pete Rose
___ **QUESTION 20:** Sparky Anderson

KEEP A RUNNING TALLY OF YOUR CORRECT ANSWERS!

Number correct: ___ / 10

Overall correct: ___ / 20

"I take my vote as a salute to the little guy, the one who doesn't hit five-hundred home runs. I was one of the guys that did all they could to win. I'm proud of my stats, but I don't think I ever got on for Joe Morgan. If I stole a base, it was to help us win a game, and I like to think that's what made me special."
— Joe Morgan, Hall of Fame Induction Speech

Joe Morgan

DALLAS GREEN WAS on the mound for the Philadelphia Phillies on September 21, 1963, when a 19-year-old kid named Joe Morgan made his major league debut in the bottom of the third inning as a pinch-hitter for Houston Colts pitcher Don Nottebart. Colts catcher John Bateman had singled to start the inning and was standing on first when Morgan stepped to the plate ... and he was still there an instant later when Morgan's debut came to a quick and rather routine end, with a harmless pop up to second baseman Tony Taylor.

If his debut was rather pedestrian, his second appearance on a big league field was more indicative of Morgan's future in the game.

One day later, with the Colts trailing 1-0 in the home half of the eighth, Johnny Temple pinch-hit and led off the inning with a walk—and Morgan was sent in to pinch-run. No, he didn't steal second to get into scoring position, and he didn't use his blazing speed to score from first on a ball hit into the gap ... instead, he took second on a sacrifice bunt by Bob Lillis and was stranded in scoring position when Hal Smith and Howie Goss struck out to end the inning. Morgan did remain in the game, however, batting eighth and playing second base—which was important, because in the bottom of the ninth the Colts began to rally. Still down 1-0, the Colts got a leadoff single from John Weekly, who was batting third in the lineup. After a failed sacrifice resulted in a fielder's choice for the first out, Jim Wynn, batting fifth, walked to move the tying run into scoring position. Batting sixth, Bob Aspromonte singled to tie the game and move the potential winning run into scoring position. After a ground out by Rusty Staub left runners at second and third with two outs, Morgan, batting eighth, stepped to the plate for the second time in his career.

And his first big league hit was a walk-off single to right field.

It came for a club that had already lost 95 games on the season and was 35 games back in the standings, fewer than

3,500 people were on hand to see it, and it was a long way from Game 7 of the World Series ... but it was clutch nonetheless, and for the rest of his career Morgan proved to be exactly that type of player.

In 1965, two years after his big league debut, Morgan was the starting second baseman for the Houston Astros. The 21-year-old full-fledged rookie placed second in Rookie of the Year balloting behind Jim Lefebvre, and for the next two decades he was one of the game's biggest stars. In November 1971, Cincinnati General Manager Bob Howsam traded Lee May, Tommy Helms, and Jimmy Stewart to Houston, and in return the Reds received Jack Billingham, César Gerónimo, Ed Armbrister, Dennis Menke ... and Joe Morgan, which prompted Sparky Anderson to tell Howsam, "You just won the Pennant for the Cincinnati Reds."

Sparky was right.

In 1972, Joe Morgan was the MVP of the All-Star Game and he led the league in runs, walks, and on-base percentage as the Reds won 95 games to claim the N.L. West, before defeating Pittsburgh in a five-game series to win the N.L. Pennant.

The Reds fell short in the World Series, however, losing in seven games to Oakland.

The 1973 postseason ended in disappointment as well, as the Mets defeated the Reds to claim the N.L. Pennant. And in 1974 the Reds were one of the best teams in baseball, winning 98 games during the regular season, however ... the Dodgers won 102 games to claim the N.L. West.

All that just set the stage for 1975.

Morgan would have his finest season to date. He batted a career high .327, led the league with 132 walks and a .466 on-base percentage, and became the third different Reds player in the 1970s to win league MVP honors. And he backed that up with a repeat MVP performance in 1976. But it was one at bat during October 1975 that defined his place in baseball history and secured the legacy of the Big Red Machine, all with one swing. After rallying from three runs down during Game 7 of the World Series at Fenway Park, it was Morgan who batted with two outs in the ninth inning of a tie game with the potential winning run in scoring position. The stakes were slightly higher than in his second career at bat, and this time there were slightly more than 35,000 fans in attendance and countless more listening and watching to the radio and TV broadcasts ... but like a dozen years earlier, Morgan was clutch. And with that game-winning hit Joe Morgan became a baseball immortal.

TOP OF THE SECOND

QUESTION 21: This Reds starter was the seventh pick overall in the 2004 amateur draft, and he was only 21-years-old when he debuted on June 8, 2007—however, it took him 30 starts over the course of three seasons before he won back-to-back games. He was only 6-12 during parts of three seasons before tossing seven strong innings in a 4-1 victory vs. Pittsburgh in 2009, and then he came back five days later to pitch his finest big league game to date—eight shutout innings vs. LA in a 4-2 victory. Who is this pitcher?
   a) Johnny Cueto
   b) Homer Bailey
   c) Danny Herrera

QUESTION 22: On July 4, 2009, this Reds starter became the first big league pitcher in over 50 years to celebrate Independence Day by hitting a home run and recording a victory. Who is this pitcher?
   a) Aaron Harang
   b) Bronson Arroyo
   c) Micah Owings

QUESTION 23: On July 7, 1993, this pitcher was fined $500 by Manager Davey Johnson because he left the ballpark during a contest at Wrigley Field. He wasn't really going AWOL, he merely went across the street and onto the rooftops looking over the legendary stadium to take in the atmosphere. Who is this pitcher?

a) Tom Browning
b) Tim Belcher
c) Bobby Ayala

QUESTION 24: On June 10, 1944, this pitcher became the youngest player in major league history when he tossed two-thirds of an inning for Cincinnati vs. the St. Louis Cardinals. He was only 15-years-old at the time. He didn't make another big league appearance until eight years later—meaning he went eight years between his first and second big league games, and yet, he was still only 23-years-old when he became a permanent fixture with the Reds in 1952. Who is this pitcher that became the youngest player in baseball history?

a) Kent Peterson
b) Joe Nuxhall
c) Jake Eisenhart

QUESTION 25: He was the first manager in franchise history—way back in 1882. Can you pick him out?

a) Will White
b) Oliver Caylor
c) Pop Snyder

QUESTION 26: On October 15, 1892, this pitcher tossed a no-hitter, the first in franchise history, in his major league debut. It was a great start to his career, but his stats for 1893: a 1-4 record with a 10.19 earned run average. And after that, well, actually that was it—he never played again. Who threw a no-hitter in his big league debut but won only two career games?

a) Charles Jones
b) Ted Breitenstein
c) Noodles Hahn

QUESTION 27: On April 22, 1898, this pitcher tossed the second no-hitter in franchise history, while that same day a pitcher named Jim Hughes tossed a no-no for Baltimore. It was the first time in baseball history that two no-hitters were tossed on the same day. Who pitched the second no-hitter in franchise history?

a) Charles Jones
b) Ted Breitenstein
c) Noodles Hahn

QUESTION 28: The Reds were dead last in 1901 with a record of 52-87, and yet this lefty won 22 games. He also completed 41 games, a modern-era record for lefties. It took 71 years before another lefty won 20-plus games for a last place team, a feat Steve Carlton accomplished for the 1972 Phillies. Who won 22 games for the last place Reds in 1901?

a) Charles Jones
b) Ted Breitenstein
c) Noodles Hahn

QUESTION 29: Okay, so this fabulous feat was actually accomplished by Cincinnati's opponent—the Atlanta Braves—but it's still pretty impressive. On May 28, 2003, Rafael Furcal, Mark DeRosa, and Gary Sheffield hit back-to-back-to-back home runs to start the game. It was only the second time in history that teammates hit three consecutive bombs leading off a game. Javy Lopez added a two-run shot later in the first. Who was the Reds pitcher that took part in this fabulous feat by serving up all four long balls?

a) Danny Graves
b) Jeff Austin
c) Paul Wilson

QUESTION 30: On September 11, 1985, Pete Rose became baseball's all-time hits leader when he singled for career hit number 4,192. Against which team did Rose record his

historic hit?
- a) Houston Astros
- b) San Diego Padres
- c) Los Angeles Dodgers

TOP OF THE SECOND ANSWER KEY

___ **QUESTION 21:** B – Homer Bailey
___ **QUESTION 22:** C – Micah Owings
___ **QUESTION 23:** A – Tom Browning
___ **QUESTION 24:** B – Joe Nuxhall
___ **QUESTION 25:** C – Pop Snyder
___ **QUESTION 26:** A – Charles Jones
___ **QUESTION 27:** B – Ted Breitenstein
___ **QUESTION 28:** C – Noodles Hahn
___ **QUESTION 29:** B – Jeff Austin
___ **QUESTION 30:** B – San Diego Padres

KEEP A RUNNING TALLY OF YOUR CORRECT ANSWERS!

Number correct: ___ / 10

Overall correct: ___ / 30

BOTTOM OF THE SECOND

QUESTION 31: On May 24, 1935, the Cincinnati Reds played host for the first major league game in history to take place under lights. The game was at Crosley Field, and Cincinnati won 2-1. Which team did the Reds beat that historic night?
   a) St. Louis Cardinals
   b) New York Giants
   c) Philadelphia Phillies

QUESTION 32: He was a seven-time All-Star for Cincinnati, and from 1938-40 he tied a record when he led the N.L. in hits for three consecutive years. He also won league MVP honors in 1940. Who was this hitting star?
   a) Ernie Lombardi
   b) Frank McCormick
   c) Billy Werber

QUESTION 33: In 2007, which Reds superstar had a 30-30 season?
   a) Ken Griffey Jr.
   b) Joey Votto
   c) Brandon Phillips

QUESTION 34: Back in 1903, one Reds pitcher actually recorded a save. Who was the star that got the only save on the roster?
   a) Noodles Hahn
   b) Bob Ewing
   c) Jack Coombs

QUESTION 35: From 1954 to 1959, the Cincinnati baseball club was referred to as the Redlegs. In 1957, who led the team in dingers?
   a) George Crowe
   b) Frank Robinson
   c) Johnny Temple

QUESTION 36: According to Wins above Replacement, who was the best player on the Reds in 1976?
a) Pete Rose
b) Joe Morgan
c) Johnny Bench

QUESTION 37: How many times did superstar shortstop Barry Larkin eclipse the 20 home run mark with the Cincinnati Reds?
a) 4
b) 2
c) 1

QUESTION 38: The 1993 season was Cincinnati's last in the N.L. West before moving to the N.L. Central. They finished the season last in the Division. Who was fired less than 50 games into the season as manager?
a) Davey Johnson
b) Lou Piniella
c) Tony Pérez

QUESTION 39: One player on the basement Reds of 1937 really liked the number 12. However, his jersey number was 1. This player hit 12 homers as well as 12 triples. Those were the highest and second highest marks on his team respectively. The 12 three-baggers were good for 3rd in the league. The two seasons before, he led the league with the numbers 18 and 14 in those same categories. Who was this player?
a) Ival Goodman
b) Kiki Cuyler
c) Dom DiMaggio

QUESTION 40: In 1915, how many more Reds players were caught stealing above the number of bases they stole successfully?
a) 0
b) 2
c) 4

BOTTOM OF THE SECOND ANSWER KEY

___ **QUESTION 31:** C – Philadelphia Phillies
___ **QUESTION 32:** B – Frank McCormick
___ **QUESTION 33:** C – Brandon Phillips
___ **QUESTION 34:** B – Bob Ewing
___ **QUESTION 35:** A – George Crowe
___ **QUESTION 36:** B – Joe Morgan
___ **QUESTION 37:** B – 2
___ **QUESTION 38:** C – Tony Pérez
___ **QUESTION 39:** A – Ival Goodman
___ **QUESTION 40:** C – 4

KEEP A RUNNING TALLY OF YOUR CORRECT ANSWERS!

Number correct: ___ / 10

Overall correct: ___ / 40

"I don't want to embarrass any other catcher by comparing him with Johnny Bench."
— Sparky Anderson

Johnny Bench

UNLIKE JOE MORGAN, Johnny Bench was drafted and came up through the Cincinnati Reds organization. It didn't take him long to reach the big leagues, either—like Morgan, his first appearance came when he was a 19-year-old kid. For Bench that was on August 28, 1967, just two years after he was the 36th overall pick in the Amateur Draft and the same season he was named the Minor League Player of the Year.

And it didn't take Bench long to have an impact at the big league level.

In 1968 he took over as the Reds starting catcher. The 20-year-old backstop batted .275 with 15 homers and 82 RBIs on the season. He made the All-Star team, won a Gold Glove, and was named the N.L. Rookie of the Year. It was the first of 13 consecutive All-Star selections for Bench, the first of ten consecutive Gold Gloves, and his Rookie of the Year recognition was just a prelude for the hardware to come.

It was after Bench's sophomore season that General Manager Bob Howsam hired Sparky Anderson as the Reds new skipper. Fans that criticized the move argued the pieces were already in place for the club to be a serious contender and those pieces should not be trusted to a rookie manager. And by "pieces" those fans were, of course, largely referring to Bench. Howsam defended his decision by stating the Reds talented young players would benefit from Anderson's leadership—and in 1970, Bench's performance on the field proved that Howsam was correct.

In the first of his two MVP seasons, Bench batted .293 and led the league with 45 home runs and 148 RBIs, giving him the league's top totals in two of the three Triple Crown categories—a feat he would do again two years later in 1972 when he batted .270 with 40 home runs and 125 RBIs to claim his second Most Valuable Player Award.

Not only was Bench one of the game's most feared sluggers, he was also a beast behind the dish. Harry Dalton, one of the game's premier front office men from the 1960s through the early 1990s, once said of Bench, "Every time Bench throws, everybody in baseball drools." And Bench wasn't lacking in confidence either at the plate or behind it. He once claimed, "I can throw out any man alive."

And he could.

After a disappointing end to the Reds 1970 postseason and an overall disappointing team campaign in 1971, Bench and the Reds geared up for another run at the postseason in 1972—and it was no surprise that after his monstrous regular season campaign it was Bench who came up with one of the biggest hits in franchise history during the deciding Game 5 of the National League Championship Series vs. the Pittsburgh Pirates. Trailing 3-2 as the game moved into the bottom of the ninth, Bench led off with an opposite field home run against Dave Giusti that tied the game 3-3. His clutch hit ignited a two-run rally that culminated with George Foster racing to the plate on a wild pitch with two outs in the inning, and the Reds claimed the Pennant in dramatic walk-off fashion. Unfortunately, the Reds momentum could carry the team only so far—and Oakland won a tense seven-game World Series.

Bench and his teammates finally closed the deal in the 1975 World Series, of course—but Bench struggled that entire postseason, batting only .077 during the NLCS vs. Pittsburgh and just .207 in the World Series vs. Boston. It was World Series MVP Pete Rose along with Joe Morgan and Tony Pérez who provided most of the heroics. And Bench's struggles continued into the 1976 regular season as the Big Red Machine attempted to repeat as World Champions. His season numbers were still good, just not what the Reds fan base was accustomed to—he batted only .234 but still hit 16 home runs with 74 RBIs, although those numbers came in a significantly reduced number of plate appearances.

That all changed when the calendar turned to October.

Just like Joe Morgan had come up clutch the year before, October 1976 was the penultimate performance of Bench's Hall of Fame career. All the early success and awards and accolades thrown in his direction had prepared him for this moment—when the Big Red Machine became a *dynasty* by *defending* it's World Championship from the season before. In the NLCS, Bench batted .333 with a home run in a three-game sweep of the Philadelphia Phillies. And then in the World Series, Bench batted .533 with eight hits and six RBIs in a four-game sweep of the Yankees. He hit two home runs in that series, both in the deciding Game 4. His two-run shot in the fourth gave the Reds a 2-1 lead, and his three-run shot in the ninth put the game away.

And for his heroics Bench earned one more serious piece of hardware: World Series MVP.

TOP OF THE THIRD

QUESTION 41: The only season from 1917-44 in which there were two no-hitters during the same season in the N.L. was 1938, and both of them were thrown in back-to-back starts by this Reds pitcher. It remains the only time in history a pitcher has thrown back-to-back no-hitters. Who pulled off that remarkable feat for the Reds in 1938?

QUESTION 42: In one of baseball's most famous home plate collisions, Pete Rose scored the game-winning run in the 12th inning to give the National League a 5-4 victory in the 1970 All-Star Game before a home crowd at Riverfront Stadium. Say what you want about Rose, but there's a reason he was called "Charlie Hustle." Can you name the All-Star catcher Rose collided with that day? The "meeting at the plate" resulted in a broken shoulder for the catcher.

QUESTION 43: Jim Maloney led the league in Ks from 1963 to 1966. In one of those years he also led the league in a dubious statistic, wild pitches. In which year did Maloney total the most wild pitches in the N.L.? It's a bonus if you can name how many of them he threw.

QUESTION 44: Which number have the Reds retired twice? As a bonus, can you tell us which two players wore that number?

QUESTION 45: The Reds swept the Athletics to win the 1990 series. So tell us, which Nasty Brother recorded the only save in the World Series? Hint: He did it in Game 4.

QUESTION 46: The Big Red Machine won 102 games and swept the Yankees in the World Series. This, of course, happened in 1976. Who jacked two homers in the clinching game?

QUESTION 47: Who had the highest career batting average with Cincinnati: Johnny Bench or Joe Morgan?

QUESTION 48: Now, let's compare those two icons more. Who had the most MVPs between the two?

QUESTION 49: This great player wore the number 13 with pride. He is the emblem of a star Red. Who is this legendary player?

QUESTION 50: In 2008, which two noteworthy Reds had the flip-flop of their records? One went 17-6 while the other went 6-17.

TOP OF THE THIRD ANSWER KEY

___ **QUESTION 41:** Johnny Vander Meer
___ **QUESTION 42:** Ray Fosse
___ **QUESTION 43:** 1963 – he threw 19
___ **QUESTION 44:** 5 – Johnny Bench and Willard Hershberger
___ **QUESTION 45:** Randy Myers
___ **QUESTION 46:** Johnny Bench
___ **QUESTION 47:** Joe Morgan (.288) – Bench (.267)
___ **QUESTION 48:** Neither, they both won the award twice
___ **QUESTION 49:** Dave Concepción
___ **QUESTION 50:** Edinson Volquez and Aaron Harang

KEEP A RUNNING TALLY OF YOUR CORRECT ANSWERS!

Number correct: ___ / 10

Overall correct: ___ / 50

BOTTOM OF THE THIRD

QUESTION 51: On May 1, 1974, Pete Rose, Joe Morgan, and Dan Driessen were the top three hitters in Cincinnati's lineup vs. Pittsburgh. The pitcher for the Pirates that day was Dock Ellis, and Rose, Morgan, and Driessen began the day against Ellis with back-to-back-to-back . . . what?
a) Intentionally hit-by-pitches
b) Ground rule doubles
c) Triples
d) Home runs

QUESTION 52: Pete Rose batted more times than any other player in history, but the all-time hit king went yard only 160 times during his career. Of Rose's 160 home runs, how many were grand slams?
a) 1
b) 3
c) 5
d) 7

QUESTION 53: This team set a major league record for most one-run victories in a season: 41. The result was 100 total victories and an N.L. Pennant. Which of the following teams won 41 one-run games?
a) 1919
b) 1939
c) 1940
d) 1961

QUESTION 54: And to follow-up on all those one-run games, only six years later this team set a major league record for most one-run *losses* in a season: also 41. The result was just 67 total victories and a sixth place finish. Which of the following teams lost 41 one-run games?
a) 1925
b) 1945

c) 1946
d) 1967

QUESTION 55: The 1919 season was the first that Cincinnati won a World Series. It was a magical year indeed as they went 96-44. Now can you answer this question ... how many pitchers on that team with at least 100 innings pitched had sub-3.00 ERAs?
a) 1
b) 0
c) 6
d) 4

QUESTION 56: Who was the only player to steal 20 bases or more for the Reds in 2010?
a) Brandon Phillips
b) Drew Stubbs
c) Willy Taveras
d) Joey Votto

QUESTION 57: Here's an interesting one sticking with the 2010 theme. Which hurler picked up eight RBIs on the year? That total was the highest on the team for all pitchers.
a) Edinson Volquez
b) Johnny Cueto
c) Bronson Arroyo
d) Homer Bailey

QUESTION 58: In 1926 the Reds had yet another winning season. Now tell me which player smacked an incredible 20 triples that year. That total was this player's career high.
a) Curt Walker
b) Wally Pipp
c) Chuck Dressen
d) Edd Roush

QUESTION 59: Just how good was Barry Larkin? His career WAR is about eleven points higher than the highest person— Tommy John—on the Veterans Election 2010 Hall of Fame ballot sheet. What is Larkin's WAR for his career?
- a) 68.8
- b) 79.7
- c) 70.2
- d) 72.5

QUESTION 60: Jim Brosnan is one of the best relievers you've probably never heard of. In 331.2 innings of play spread out across five seasons, what was his ERA while in Cincy?
- a) 2.87
- b) 3.04
- c) 4.92
- d) 3.17

Bottom of the Third Answer Key

___ **Question 51:** A – Ellis hit all three intentionally
___ **Question 52:** A – only 1, on July 18, 1964, vs. Dallas Green, who later was Rose's manager in Philadelphia
___ **Question 53:** C – 1940
___ **Question 54:** C – 1946
___ **Question 55:** C – 6
___ **Question 56:** B – Drew Stubbs
___ **Question 57:** C – Bronson Arroyo
___ **Question 58:** A – Curt Walker
___ **Question 59:** A – 68.8
___ **Question 60:** B – 3.04

Keep a running tally of your correct answers!

Number correct: ___ / 10

Overall correct: ___ / 60

"Somebody's gotta win and somebody's gotta lose and I believe in letting the other guy lose."
— Pete Rose

Pete Rose

THERE'S A REASON people called baseball's all-time hits leader Charlie Hustle—and it's really simple, no one worked harder, played harder, or cared more about his team winning than did Pete Rose. And while it is true that the moniker Charlie Hustle was used by peers early in Rose's career to take jabs at him, insinuating that he lacked the same talent as most major league players and therefore he *had* to work harder than everyone else, it is also true that because Rose worked and played so hard that kids all across the country—not just in Cincinnati—were emulating him on sandlots everywhere, proud to dirty their jerseys doing a headfirst "Pete Rose" dive into cardboard boxes used for bases ... whether they needed to slide or not.

You can fault Rose for decisions he made post-playing career that thus far have kept him out of Cooperstown, but there's no denying his passion for the game or the contribution made by the Cincinnati native to the building and ultimate success of the Big Red Machine.

Rose signed as an amateur free agent with Cincinnati in 1960 and just three years later was starting for the big club. The 22-year-old rookie second baseman walked in his first big league at bat, but it wasn't until his fourth game, on April 13, 1963, that Rose collected his first big league hit. After starting the season 0 for 11, Rose hit a triple off Pittsburgh's Bob Friend for his first major league hit. It took Rose 15 games before he had a multi-hit game, going 2 for 5 vs. St. Louis on May 4 to raise his average from .186 to .222. After that he found his groove, collecting multiple hits in five of his next ten games to raise his average to .278, and you could argue from that point forward that Rose never looked back. For the season Rose batted .273 with 25 doubles and a team leading 101 runs—and his strong play earned him N.L. Rookie of the Year honors.

In 1965, Rose led the league with 209 hits. The man who would one day eclipse Ty Cobb as baseball's all-time hits leader would go on to lead the league in hits six times during his time with the Reds.

In 1968, Rose batted .335 to win his first batting title. He defended it the very next season by batting a career high .348. And then in 1973 he put together his finest season— setting a career high with a league best 230 hits and winning his third batting title with a .338 average. Rose also scored 115 runs and earned N.L. Most Valuable Player honors.

And despite all this success, his greatest moments were yet to come.

In 1975, Rose led the league with 47 doubles and 112 runs—and the 34-year-old third baseman, having moved to the hot corner to enable more playing time for George Foster, also led the team with a .317 average, .406 on-base percentage, and 210 hits. Rose drew 89 walks that season but struck out only 50 times. And after a dozen years with the club and three trips to the postseason—all of which ended in disappointment— perhaps no one in the organization was more focused or motivated to finish 1975 with a victory than Pete Rose.

In the NLCS he batted .357 with a home run as the Reds swept the Pirates. And then in the World Series vs. Boston he batted .370 with a series leading ten hits. In the deciding Game 7, Boston led 3-2 in the top of the seventh inning when Rose stepped to the plate vs. Bill Lee with two on and two out. His single to center field scored Ken Griffey with the tying run, setting the stage for Joe Morgan's ninth inning heroics.

As the team sprayed champagne in the clubhouse, it was Rose who was named World Series MVP.

For Rose, he was only at the midpoint of an extraordinary career and there were many great moments yet to come. On May 5, 1978, he collected his 3,000th career hit vs. Montreal pitcher Steve Rogers. Nearly every player who has reached that plateau did so at the end of his career with his major accomplishments firmly in the rearview mirror—not so for Rose. Most people forget that it was *after* collecting his 3,000th hit that Rose began his 44-game hitting streak on June 14, 1978. Three years later, as a member of the Philadelphia Phillies, Rose led the league in hits for the seventh and final time—*and he was 40 years old.* On April 13, 1984, Rose doubled vs. Philadelphia's Jerry Koosman for his 4,000th career hit—and then on September 11, 1985, he singled vs. San Diego's Eric Show to break Ty Cobb's all-time record with his 4,192nd career hit.

And yet ... without question, it was October 22, 1975, that defined Pete Rose's career—Game 7 vs. Boston, a clutch two-out, game-tying single that led to a World Championship. For all the individual records he set and awards he accumulated, the only reason Pete Rose played the game was *to win*, and it was his passion and desire that fueled the Big Red Machine.

TOP OF THE FOURTH

QUESTION 61: The number 13 proved to be bad luck for the Reds in 1913. Joe Tinker managed them to a .418 winning percentage—which is nothing good. What was so special about him? Besides him getting fired of course.
- a) He got suspended for getting into a fight
- b) He ate ten hot dogs before each game
- c) He was also a player
- d) Nothing, he was just a terrible manager

QUESTION 62: Let's keep reliving that wonderful sweep of the Yanks in 1976. Who was credited with the win in Game 4?
- a) Jim Maloney
- b) Gary Nolan
- c) Ed Figueroa
- d) Will McEnaney

QUESTION 63: This will get a laugh out of you. For those that don't know, Francisco Cordero's agent is ... Bean Stringfellow! What a name! Anyway, how much money did Stringfellow string out of the Reds to give to Cordero in 2010?
- a) $5 million
- b) $15 million

c) $8 million
d) $12 million

QUESTION 64: Aaron Harang's best season came in 2007. In that year, what statistic made him an N.L. leader?
a) Innings pitched
b) Strikeouts
c) Strikeout to Walk Ratio
d) WAR

QUESTION 65: Who is the only player on the active major league roster of the Cincinnati Reds to have been taken in the Rule 5 Draft?
a) Jared Burton
b) Joey Votto
c) Ramón Hernández
d) Bronson Arroyo

QUESTION 66: How many batters in the everyday starting lineup were lefties on the 2010 Reds?
a) 0
b) 2
c) 4
d) 1

QUESTION 67: According to dWAR—a statistic that measures wins above replacement for defensive stats—which of the following was a better fielder for the 2010 Reds? This may surprise you a bit.
a) Jay Bruce
b) Joey Votto
c) Orlando Cabrera
d) Brandon Phillips

QUESTION 68: Now according to dWAR, who was the worst fielder on the 2010 Cincinnati Reds?

a) Ryan Hanigan
b) Ramón Hernández
c) Joey Votto
d) Jonny Gomes

QUESTION 69: Making $12.5 million in 2010, who was the Reds highest paid player that year?
a) Joey Votto
b) Aaron Harang
c) Brandon Phillips
d) Bronson Arroyo

QUESTION 70: Out of all pitchers with at least 100 innings thrown, who led the 1928 Cincinnati Reds in ERA?
a) Ray Kolp
b) Eppa Rixey
c) Jim Maloney
d) Carl Mays

TOP OF THE FOURTH ANSWER KEY

___ **QUESTION 61:** C – He was also a player
___ **QUESTION 62:** B – Gary Nolan
___ **QUESTION 63:** D – 12 million
___ **QUESTION 64:** C – Strikeout to Walk Ratio
___ **QUESTION 65:** A – Jared Burton
___ **QUESTION 66:** B – 2
___ **QUESTION 67:** A – Jay Bruce
___ **QUESTION 68:** D – Jonny Gomes
___ **QUESTION 69:** B – Aaron Harang
___ **QUESTION 70:** A – Ray Kolp

KEEP A RUNNING TALLY OF YOUR CORRECT ANSWERS!

Number correct: ___ / 10

Overall correct: ___ / 70

BOTTOM OF THE FOURTH

QUESTION 71: On October 14, 1995, the Atlanta Braves swept the Cincinnati Reds in the NLCS. That's nothing to be ashamed of when you think of how far they came, and the formidable foes they faced. Which reliever gave up five earned runs in that game for the Reds?
   a) Mark Wohlers
   b) Rob Dibble
   c) Michael Jackson
   d) Dave Burba

QUESTION 72: Joe Nuxhall had his number retired by the Reds as a broadcaster, and everybody knows that he is the youngest player to debut in a game. With the Reds in 1955, what category did he lead the league in with five of this stat?
   a) Complete games
   b) Losses
   c) Walks
   d) Shutouts

QUESTION 73: What rank was Dave Collins in stolen bases in 1980 in the N.L.? He had 79 swiped bags.
   a) 1st
   b) 2nd
   c) 3rd
   d) 4th

QUESTION 74: Not only did right fielder Austin Kearns have the highest WAR on the 2002 Reds, 4.1, what did he do that nobody else on the team did that year?
   a) Stole 40 bases
   b) Hit 40 homers
   c) Hit over .300
   d) Had 80 RBIs

QUESTION 75: Teams take time before they can win a World Series. In 1989, the year before the Reds World Series win,

what place did they finish in their Division?
- a) Sixth
- b) First
- c) Second
- d) Fifth

QUESTION 76: Who has the most Opening Day starts in Cincinnati Reds history?
- a) Aaron Harang
- b) Mario Soto
- c) Jose Rijo
- d) Pete Donohue

QUESTION 77: Staying with that, which Reds icon has the highest total number of Opening Day starts at any position?
- a) Johnny Bench
- b) Joe Morgan
- c) Barry Larkin
- d) Dave Concepción

QUESTION 78: C'mon, everybody knows that Sparky Anderson was the manager of the Big Red Machine ... but do you remember who the GM was?
- a) Thomas Newman
- b) Bill DeWitt
- c) Dick Wagner
- d) Bob Howsam

QUESTION 79: In what year did Cincy have its highest payroll?
- a) 2008
- b) 2009
- c) 2010
- d) 1976

QUESTION 80: In what year did the Reds have the highest attendance?

a) 1990
b) 2010
c) 1976
d) 2008

Bottom of the Fourth Answer Key

___ **Question 71:** C – Michael Jackson
___ **Question 72:** D – Shutouts
___ **Question 73:** C – 3rd
___ **Question 74:** C – Hit over .300
___ **Question 75:** D – Fifth
___ **Question 76:** B – Mario Soto
___ **Question 77:** C – Barry Larkin
___ **Question 78:** D – Bob Howsam
___ **Question 79:** A – 2008
___ **Question 80:** C – 1976

Keep a running tally of your correct answers!

Number correct: ___ / 10

Overall correct: ___ / 80

"In the summer of 1977, there was no more feared hitter in baseball than George Foster."
— Cincinnati Reds Hall of Fame Exhibit

George Foster

JOE MORGAN WON league MVP honors in 1976 for the second consecutive season, but the Big Red Machine was so finely tuned and dominant that year that four of the top eight in MVP balloting were from the Reds starting lineup: Morgan, George Foster (2nd), Pete Rose (4th), and Ken Griffey (8th). A quick check of the league's offensive leaders gives an even better indication of how powerful the club's offense was: Morgan led the league in on-base and slugging percentage, Morgan was also second in steals, RBIs, extra-base hits, and times on base; Rose was fourth in the league in batting and third in on-base percentage, but he led the league in runs, hits, doubles, and times on base, and he was second in total bases; Foster was second only to Morgan in slugging percentage, he was ninth in runs and tenth in hits, but he was third in total bases and fourth in home runs, and he led the league with 121 RBIs and was third in extra-base hits; add Ken Griffey to the mix and he was second in batting and among the top ten in on-base percentage, runs, hits, triples, steals, and times on base.

In other words, the Big Red Machine was exactly that—a freaking machine.

The Reds 1976 offense led the league with 857 runs, 1,599 hits, 271 doubles, 63 triples, 141 home runs, 210 steals, 681 walks, .280 average, .357 on-base percentage, .424 slugging percentage, and 2,419 total bases. That's a complete sweep of every significant offensive statistic that was kept in 1976—the Reds were the best in the league in every one of them.

As the Machine embarked on 1977 and its quest for a three-peat, fans and media alike gave their attention to Rose and Morgan and Bench—but by mid-summer, that would change.

George Foster made his big league debut for the San Francisco Giants on September 10, 1969. After short late-season stints with the Giants in 1969 and 1970, Foster finally broke through for his first full season in the majors in 1971—but that same season, on May 29, he was traded to Cincinnati for Frank Duffy and Vern Geishert. He played 104 games for the Reds that season, but the next two years combined for just 76 games at the big league level. It wasn't until 1975 that he began to get consistent playing time and started producing consistent power numbers for the Cincinnati Reds.

His timing could not have been better.

Foster set career highs, batting .300 with 23 home runs and 78 RBIs for the 1975 World Championship club. He backed up that campaign with career highs again for the 1976 World Championship club, batting .306 with 29 home runs and 121 RBIs.

The Big Red Machine came back to earth offensively in 1977—but not George Foster, what he did was insane.

The club had led the league in every category the year before, but in 1977 did not lead the league in any statistically significant category. The offense was still second in runs, third in hits and home runs, and second in batting, on-base percentage, and slugging, but its gaudy presence across all the leader boards was less pervasive than 1976.

Not true for Foster.

He set career highs for the third consecutive season … and he nearly won the Triple Crown.

Foster began 1977 in solid fashion, although not yet prolific. He batted .329 in the season's first month, but hit just three home runs in 19 games—although he did drive home 20. In May, however, the opposite was true—Foster hit eight home runs and had 13 extra-base hits in 25 games, but added only 11 RBIs to his total.

It was in June that his stats became prolific, and media and fans everywhere stood up and took notice.

Foster batted .333 in 28 games, collecting 38 hits, eight doubles, nine home runs, and 38 RBIs. He reached the All-Star break batting .316 with 29 home runs and 90 RBIs.

Foster belted 12 homers in July and 12 more in August, and by September he was clearly going to win the home run and RBIs titles—but he trailed Dave Parker, who at the time was with the Pirates, significantly for the batting title. Foster hit eight more home runs in September and he also batted .371 for the month to raise his average to .320, and at the same time Parker began to struggle and his average began to drop ... but not enough. Parker finished at .338 to claim the batting title, and Foster finished fourth in that race.

Foster's pursuit of history also played out against the backdrop of a Pennant race. The Reds were in second place to the Dodgers virtually the entire season, but after winning 12 of 15 in late August it looked like the Reds were going to make a run at defending their title. It wasn't to be, however—after dropping 5 of 6 to open September, the only drama left was Foster's pursuit of history.

Could he win the Triple Crown?

Could he hit 60 home runs?

Well, no ... but he hardly failed. The landslide N.L. MVP that season, Foster finished with a league best 124 runs, 52 homers, 149 RBIs, .631 slugging percentage, and 388 total bases. It was the sixth time in eight seasons that league MVP honors went to a member of the Big Red Machine—two for Bench, two for Morgan, and one each for Rose and Foster.

Today, Foster lacks the name recognition outside of Cincinnati that other members of the Big Red machine maintain, but that doesn't diminish his contributions to the club—he followed his MVP campaign with three more seasons of 20-plus home runs and 90-plus RBIs, never mind the fact he batted .326 during three trips to the World Series. And just like Rose and Morgan and Bench during their MVP seasons, Foster can say, if only for that one summer, he was the best in the game.

TOP OF THE FIFTH

QUESTION 81: Who has the highest OPS in Reds history?
    a)   Frank Robinson
    b)   Joey Votto
    c)   Johnny Bench
    d)   Joe Morgan

QUESTION 82: In 1991, who did the Cincinnati Reds select with their first-round pick in the Amateur Draft?
    a)   Barry Larkin
    b)   Austin Kearns
    c)   Nick Esasky
    d)   Pokey Reese

QUESTION 83: What was so interesting about the Reds vs. Cardinals game on April 6, 1994?
    a)   Barry Larkin had his 3000th hit
    b)   They tied
    c)   The Reds won by 20 runs
    d)   Tom Browning tossed a No-Hitter

QUESTION 84: Everybody knows that Deion Sanders is the best defensive back in NFL history. Everyone also knows that Prime Time took his skills to the diamond too. Which big star did the Reds mistakenly deal to the Braves for Deion? As good as Deion was on the gridiron and in a couple of MLB seasons, he was absolutely horrid with the Reds. By the way, this deal went down on May 29, 1994.
    a)   Barry Larkin
    b)   Ray Lankford
    c)   Roberto Kelly
    d)   Brett Boone

QUESTION 85: Who smashed 40 dingers and walked 112 times in 2006 for the Cincinnati Reds? He led the Reds in five major stat categories that year.

a) Adam Dunn
b) Brandon Phillips
c) Austin Kearns
d) Ken Griffey Jr.

QUESTION 86: Who has the highest WAR in a single season in Reds franchise history with 12? He scored 107 runs, had 94 RBIs, swiped 67 bags, and drew 132 walks while striking out only 52 times. He also hit .327, had an OBP of .466, slugged .508, and had a .974 OPS. Yeah, this is the stuff of a legend because it is one!
a) Frank Robinson
b) Barry Larkin
c) Joe Morgan
d) Johnny Bench

QUESTION 87: How many World Series titles have the Reds won?
a) 1
b) 2
c) 3
d) 5

QUESTION 88: The Cincinnati Reds have had huge stars such as Joe Morgan, Jose Rijo, and Johnny Bench, all of which helped the Reds to the postseason. How many Pennants has Cincy won in franchise history?
a) 7
b) 10
c) 9
d) 14

QUESTION 89: In 2010 the Reds won 91 games—the last time the Reds had won 90-plus games was during which year?
a) 1976
b) 1990

    c) 2005
    d) 1999

QUESTION 90: In 1993, what Division were the Cincinnati Reds a part of?
    a) N.L. Central
    b) A.L. Central
    c) N.L. East
    d) N.L. West

TOP OF THE FIFTH ANSWER KEY

___ **QUESTION 81:** B – Joey Votto
___ **QUESTION 82:** D – Pokey Reese
___ **QUESTION 83:** B – They tied
___ **QUESTION 84:** C – Roberto Kelly
___ **QUESTION 85:** A – Adam Dunn
___ **QUESTION 86:** C – Joe Morgan
___ **QUESTION 87:** D – 5
___ **QUESTION 88:** B – 10
___ **QUESTION 89:** D – 1999
___ **QUESTION 90:** D – N.L. West

KEEP A RUNNING TALLY OF YOUR CORRECT ANSWERS!

Number correct: ___ / 10

Overall correct: ___ / 90

BOTTOM OF THE FIFTH

QUESTION 91: It was a dismal season in 1982 as the Reds lost 101 games. Who led the team in WAR that year?
a) Johnny Bench
b) Ron Oester
c) Mario Soto
d) Charlie Leibrandt

QUESTION 92: In 1955, this star duo for the Reds combined to bash 87 homers. Who were these powerful studs? One hit 47 dingers, the other hit 40.
a) Johnny Bench and Joe Morgan
b) Johnny Temple and Smoky Burgess
c) Roy McMillan and Rocky Bridges
d) Ted Kluszewski and Wally Post

QUESTION 93: How many RBIs did Greasy Neale—who was better known for his steals—have in his career with the Reds?
a) 500
b) 199
c) 250
d) 138

QUESTION 94: Sherry Magee was one of the best players in MLB history, and he happened to spend the dwindling years of his incredible career in Cincinnati. His next to last year was 1918, but by no means was this great washed-up or done with his feats yet. What statistic did he lead the N.L. in during the 1918 season?
a) Batting average
b) Walks
c) RBIs
d) Homers

QUESTION 95: What did Willy Mo Pena do in 2004 with the Reds that he never did for the rest of his career?

a) 80 or more RBIs
b) 20 or more home runs
c) 20 or more stolen bases
d) Hit .290 or more

QUESTION 96: Edd Roush accomplished which great feat in 1924?
a) 20 or more triples
b) He hit .375 or more
c) He smashed 50 or more dingers
d) He didn't get a hit in 40 or more at bats

QUESTION 97: In 1941, Bucky Walters tossed five shutouts and 27 complete games, had a 2.83 ERA, and won 19 games. What else did Walters do?
a) Accumulate over 200 strikeouts
b) Pitched over 300 innings
c) Won a World Series ring
d) Was promoted to player-manager

QUESTION 98: Johnny Vander Meer is a huge icon in Reds history. What was his career ERA with the Reds?
a) 3.74
b) 2.91
c) 3.57
d) 3.44

QUESTION 99: Vander Meer led the N.L. in which category for three straight years?
a) Innings pitched
b) Walks
c) Strikeouts
d) ERA

QUESTION 100: When was the Reds franchise made?
a) 1901
b) 1882

c) 1898
d) 1867

Bottom of the Fifth Answer Key

__ **Question 91:** C – Mario Soto
__ **Question 92:** D – Ted Kluszewski and Wally Post
__ **Question 93:** B – 199
__ **Question 94:** C – RBIs
__ **Question 95:** B – 20 or more home runs
__ **Question 96:** A – 20 or more triples
__ **Question 97:** B – Pitched over 300 innings
__ **Question 98:** D – 3.44
__ **Question 99:** C – Strikeouts
__ **Question 100:** B – 1882

Keep a running tally of your correct answers!

Number correct: __ / 10

Overall correct: __ / 100

"A catalyst of Cincinnati's talented Big Red Machine teams during the 1970s, his subtle leadership and timely hitting helped pace those clubs to five Division titles, four Pennants, and two World Series championships."
— Tony Pérez's Baseball Hall of Fame Plaque

Tony Pérez

THE BIG RED Machine was a star-studded collection of players to be sure, but perhaps the finest compliment given to any one member of that group was when Sparky Anderson referred to Tony Pérez as its de facto leader. The Hall of Fame legend, who hails from Cuba, was a seven-time All-Star and the MVP of the 1967 All-Star Game … but surprisingly, despite playing all or parts of 23 seasons in the big leagues, Pérez was never a league MVP and he never led the league in any statistically significant category.

Well, almost never.

He did lead the league in grounding into double plays once … but home runs? RBIs? Extra-base hits?

No, no, and no.

So how is it that Sparky, one of the game's all-time great managers, would point to Pérez as being the guy leading the Big Red Machine?

Easy—Pérez was *clutch.*

Pérez hit the century mark in RBIs six times and he had back-to-back seasons with 37 and 40 home runs respectively, and with career totals of 379 bombs, 1,652 RBIs, and 963 extra-base hits, he easily ranks among baseball's top 75 all-time in all three categories, despite never being the league's best for a single season. And yet none of that is why Pérez stood out to his teammates and his manager.

Pérez stood out because he was a clutch hitter.

And like Bench and Morgan and Rose, it was a clutch October hit that immortalized him in baseball's postseason lore. The powerful first baseman hit three home runs against Boston during the 1975 World Series, but none bigger than his blast against Bill Lee.

It was Game 7, and Boston led 3-0 in the sixth inning.

In his book, Lee described what happened next this way: "I had been having good success with Tony, throwing him my slow, arching curveball, so I thought it would be a good idea to throw it to him again. Unfortunately, so did Tony, who timed it beautifully. He counted the seams of the ball as it floated up to the plate, checked to see if Lee MacPhail's signature was on it, signed his own name to it, and then jumped all over it."

The blast over the Green Monster made it a 3-2 ballgame and set the stage for the late-inning heroics of Rose and Morgan.

It was clutch.

Pérez had signed with Cincinnati as a teenager in 1960, and he debuted for the club on July 26, 1964, which meant 1975 was the third trip to the World Series that he made with the Reds. He'd get one more—he was there for the repeat in 1976, but the 34-year-old veteran was traded to Montreal that December.

In 1983, Pérez would make one final trip to the World Series, this time with the Philadelphia Phillies—also on that team were Pete Rose and Joe Morgan.

Coincidence?

Not so much.

Confident players and clutch performers lead to success ... which serves only to breed more success. Not really a surprise that veteran leadership won a couple of Pennants for the Phillies during that time, after all, the Big Red Machine began its decline *after* the trade of Pérez. The offense was still dominant and the Reds were still a spectacular ballclub ... but there was no longer the separation between the Reds and the rest of the league that was there at the height of the Machine.

And there were no more postseason trips for the Reds with Sparky at the helm.

All baseball dynasties end, of course—but what came after the trade of Pérez proved Sparky Anderson's assertion regarding his status among that star-studded collection of players we know and love as the Big Red Machine to be correct: the Hall of Fame first baseman was it's clutch leader.

TOP OF THE SIXTH

QUESTION 101: Adam Dunn just signed a four-year deal worth $56 million with the Chicago White Sox. However, Reds fans will immortally remember him. Dunn has already entered the legends discussion, having slammed 354 dingers in ten seasons. How many did he hit during eight seasons with the Reds? By the way, for those mathematicians out there, that's 35.4 dingers per year. Nice, huh?
    a) 298
    b) 305
    c) 270
    d) 289

QUESTION 102: As you know, Barry Larkin is still looking to find his name on the list of Hall of Famers. This is once again a year where Larkin will be on the ballot, and he has my full vote. How many Gold Glove Awards did this star shortstop add to his trophy case? Yeah, I know some people say that Gold Glove Awards are overrated—but if anyone deserved them, Larkin did.
    a) 6
    b) 3
    c) 5
    d) 8

QUESTION 103: Who managed the Reds in 1991?
    a) Dusty Baker
    b) Sparky Anderson
    c) Hal Morris
    d) Lou Piniella

QUESTION 104: The 1972 season was great for Gary Nolan. How low was this Reds starter's ERA?
    a) 1.99
    b) 2.07

c) 3.01
d) 2.36

QUESTION 105: How did the Reds acquire Joe Morgan?
a) Amateur Draft
b) Free agency
c) Trade
d) He just appeared by way of the baseball gods

QUESTION 106: In 1933 the Reds were last in the league. Which legend was the only Red who hit double digits in homers? Yeah, that's pretty sad. Cincy can't blame the dead ball era for that one.
a) Hobe Ferris
b) Noodles Hahn
c) Leo Durocher
d) Jim Bottomley

QUESTION 107: Getting swept by the 2010 Phillies isn't such a bad thing. Especially when it took beating the heavily favored Cardinals for the Division title through the regular season to get to the postseason. Aroldis Chapman, the rookie fireballer from Cuba, was all the talk. The Reds made a splash to get him. It took 5 years and 30 million, but the young and promising pitcher was theirs. Now how do these two things tie in? Well, what did Chapman do in Game 2 of the NLDS in an appearance out of the pen?
a) Blown save
b) Hold
c) Three straight Ks
d) Save

QUESTION 108: Junior, the Kid, Griff. Call him what you'd like. The man with 600 homers has been long famed for his power, strong character, speed, and defensive skills. He also didn't take steroids in the steroid era—but he did take untimely naps. Let's just say that he is a true baseball player and one of the few heroes left. The sad thing is, Ken Griffey Jr. could have been better than Barry Bonds and A-Rod had he not endured so many injuries. How many homers did Griff hit during nine seasons with the Reds? Clue, he hit 417 in 13 seasons with the Ms.

a) 278
b) 198
c) 210
d) 303

QUESTION 109: Sean Casey has always been a Reds favorite. How many All-Star teams did he make for the Reds? The fans really did like him.

a) 7
b) 3
c) 5
d) 9

QUESTION 110: Sean Casey ended his career with the Reds in 2005 on a bad note. He was a good player in Cincinnati, but he did something that just doesn't bode well. What did ol' Casey do this time?

a) Not hit double digit homers
b) Led the league in times caught stealing
c) Punched the ump on the last game of the season
d) Led the league in double plays

TOP OF THE SIXTH ANSWER KEY

___ **QUESTION 101:** C – 270
___ **QUESTION 102:** B – 3
___ **QUESTION 103:** D – Lou Piniella
___ **QUESTION 104:** A – 1.99
___ **QUESTION 105:** C – Trade
___ **QUESTION 106:** D – Jim Bottomley
___ **QUESTION 107:** A – Blown save
___ **QUESTION 108:** C – 210
___ **QUESTION 109:** B – 3
___ **QUESTION 110:** D – Led the league in double plays

KEEP A RUNNING TALLY OF YOUR CORRECT ANSWERS!

Number correct: ___ / 10

Overall correct: ___ / 110

BOTTOM OF THE SIXTH

QUESTION 111: Pokey Reese made just 270K in 1999. That's no surprise considering this is pre-A-Rod big contract time, and it was his third season in the league. Reese gave the Reds every quarter-penny of that deal. He scored 85 runs, hit 37 doubles, hit five triples, and stole 38 bases. They weren't out of the world numbers, but they were pretty good. Besides, that's worth far more than $270,000. Don't you think? Anyway, what award did he win in 1999?
  a) Silver Slugger
  b) Gold Glove
  c) Sterling Shortstop
  d) Reds MVP

QUESTION 112: Who was the Reds player-manager in 1908?
  a) Sparky Anderson
  b) Noodles Hahn
  c) John Ganzel
  d) Mike Mitchell

QUESTION 113: In 1903, Mike Donlin was absolutely spectacular. He hit 18 triples, scored 110 runs, stole 26 bases, had an OBP of .420, slugged .516, and had an OPS of .936. These are great stats for the dead ball era. However, none of them were his best stat. What significant statistical achievement—because baseball is all about the stats, unlike soccer—did he achieve in 1903?
  a) .351 batting average
  b) 15 homers
  c) 20 homers
  d) 49 doubles

QUESTION 114: The 1981 Cincinnati Reds won the N.L. West with a .611 winning percentage. In 108 games—not 162, thanks to the work stoppage—the Reds went 66-42 with John McNamara at the helm. They weren't exactly friends with

power that year. Which man was the only person to hit (at least) 20 homers, 90 RBIs, slug .500, and have an OPS of .800? They certainly proved you don't need power to win Division titles. Well who was the only Red that showed power in '81?
   a) George Foster
   b) Johnny Bench
   c) Ken Griffey
   d) Dave Concepción

QUESTION 115: How many times did Eppa Rixey lead the N.L. in games started while with the Cincinnati Reds?
   a) 2
   b) 1
   c) 5
   d) 3

QUESTION 116: Don Newcombe won the first ever Cy Young Award—along with an MVP award—in his mind-boggling 1956 campaign. He had one nice season with the Reds in 1959 before being traded to Cleveland. What statistic did he lead the league in during his last full season in Cincinnati?
   a) Walks per nine innings
   b) Strikeouts
   c) Innings pitched
   d) Wins

QUESTION 117: What was star pitcher Ray Kolp's nickname?
   a) Bowl of Kolp
   b) Jockey
   c) Crab
   d) Ray-K

QUESTION 118: Hall of Fame outfielder Kiki Cuyler spent the last two and a half seasons of his career in Cincinnati. One year, he scored 96 runs, hit 11 triples, batted .326, and had 185 total hits. He was 37 years old that year. Well, what year was it? Don't worry, you don't need the speed that it takes to hit a

Nolan Ryan fastball ... take your time.
  a) 1947
  b) 1924
  c) 1936
  d) 1941

QUESTION 119: How many Cy Young Awards did George Suggs win?
  a) 3
  b) 1
  c) 2
  d) 0

QUESTION 120: Harry Heilmann is a HOFer who spent the last two seasons of his famed career with the Reds. Heilmann once hit .403 in a season. What was his nickname?
  a) Heelman
  b) Hairy
  c) Slug
  d) Clip

Bottom of the Sixth Answer Key

___ **Question 111:** B – Gold Glove
___ **Question 112:** C – John Ganzel
___ **Question 113:** A – .351 batting average
___ **Question 114:** A – George Foster
___ **Question 115:** A – 2
___ **Question 116:** A – Walks per nine innings
___ **Question 117:** B – Jockey
___ **Question 118:** C – 1936
___ **Question 119:** D – 0
___ **Question 120:** C – Slug

Keep a running tally of your correct answers!

Number correct: ___ / 10

Overall correct: ___ / 120

"Maybe somewhere there has been a man who played shortstop as well as he does, but I assure you there has never been a man who can cover the amount of ground he covers."
— Sparky Anderson

Dave Concepción

THE CINCINNATI REDS signed a scrawny, scrappy teenage Venezuelan prospect in 1967. He obviously had talent, but no one could have foreseen that he would one day be a member of the Cincinnati Reds Hall of Fame, or that he would retire after a 19-year career that established a franchise record for continuous service with the club, or that he'd be an invaluable member to a Machine that won six Division titles, four Pennants, and two World Championships.

Dave Concepción exceeded everyone's expectations—everyone's except, perhaps, his own. That's because as a kid, Concepción idolized Major League Hall of Fame shortstop and fellow-Venezuelan Luis Aparicio, and he aspired to become that same caliber of player.

Cincinnati signed him, however, to play second base.

No problem. In 1968, his work ethic, strong arm, and desire led minor league skipper George Scherger to move him to shortstop—never mind the fact the Reds already had two highly prized shortstop prospects in Frank Duffy and Darrel Chaney. But the experiment was so successful that when rookie skipper Sparky Anderson took over in 1970, he included Concepción on his Opening Day roster. A year later, Duffy was traded to the Giants for George Foster, and Chaney spent the next five years as a utility infielder for the Reds until he was finally traded to the Atlanta Braves.

Concepción had, meanwhile, not so quietly become one of the premier shortstops of the 1970s—and "not so quietly" isn't a reference to his disposition, but rather to the fact that he was constantly performing at the highest levels on baseball's biggest stages: the Mid-Summer Classic and October Baseball. His breakout season was 1973, when he batted .414 during the first two weeks of the season. Concepción's strong start continued through the mid-summer and he earned a spot on his first All-Star team—batting .287 with eight home runs during the season's first half. The league had already taken notice of his slick fielding, aggressive base running, and ability to steal bases, but for the first time in his career Concepción was just as dangerous to his opponent's when he was batting.

Unfortunately, he broke his ankle on July 22 while sliding into third, and his season came to an abrupt end.

Undeterred, Concepción came back in 1974 and earned his first of five Gold Gloves. He teamed with second baseman Joe Morgan to form one of the most fluid and extraordinary double play combinations in baseball history. And as the decade moved on, and the Big Red Machine plowed through its opponents, Concepción kept getting better.

In addition to his Gold Gloves, he won two Silver Slugger Awards and was a nine-time All-Star—and he won MVP honors in the 1982 Mid-Summer Classic.

Concepción also played in nine postseason series, totaling 34 games. He batted .297 with 30 hits—nine for extra-bases—13 runs, 13 RBIs, and seven steals. Cincinnati was 6-3 during the postseason series in which he played.

In 2000 he was inducted into the Reds Hall of Fame. You could make a strong argument that he belongs in Cooperstown as well—nonetheless, Reds fans understand and appreciate his place in franchise history. When you look at the rosters that made up the Big Red Machine, you can't cross off any names and assert the team would have been just as strong and won just as much without a particular player—but for sure, you can look at a name like Concepción and assert that *without* him, it's unlikely that today we'd be writing about a team known as the Big Red Machine.

TOP OF THE SEVENTH

QUESTION 121: Dusty Baker has an interesting name and is also one of the league's premier managers. He has managed the Giants, Cubs, and Reds. He has yet to win a Manager of the Year Award with his current team—he was robbed of it this past year—but how many Manager of the Year Awards has Baker won in his career?

a) 3
b) 0
c) 2
d) 1

QUESTION 122: Who was the only .300 hitter for the Reds in 2009?
a) Brandon Phillips
b) Ken Griffey Jr.
c) Jay Bruce
d) Joey Votto

QUESTION 123: Bronson Arroyo won 15 games and pitched 220.1 innings in a typical Bronson Arroyo season. How many complete games did he toss?
a) 2
b) 3
c) 1
d) 5

QUESTION 124: Homer Bailey was once regarded as one of the best pitching prospects in baseball. He has underachieved, but he showed bright spots in 2010. His strikeouts per nine innings ratio was 8.3. How many strikeouts did he record?
a) 146
b) 100
c) 200
d) 89

QUESTION 125: Frank Robinson was a 22-year-old third-year player in 1958 ... and yet he led the team in home runs for the second time in three seasons. How many home runs did he hit in 1958?
a) 29
b) 31
c) 36
d) 39

QUESTION 126: Through 2010, how many Hall of Famers have played for the Reds?

    a) 27
    b) 39
    c) 33
    d) 10

QUESTION 127: Who was the only pitcher to record 200 strikeouts for the 2007 Cincinnati Reds?

    a) Aaron Harang
    b) Bronson Arroyo
    c) Johnny Cueto
    d) Kyle Lohse

QUESTION 128: David Weathers isn't exactly closer material. He's a good set-up man, but that doesn't equate to being a good closer. However, he did lead the league in games finished with 60 of them in 2007. How many saves did he have in his first and final year of closing?

    a) 15
    b) 22
    c) 33
    d) 45

QUESTION 129: Bronson Arroyo is one of the steadiest pitchers in baseball. Sure he took steroids, but at least he had the guts to admit it right off without being investigated. Anyway, where did he place in the Cy Young balloting in 2010? Yes, he actually did get some votes.

    a) 7th
    b) 22nd
    c) 16th
    d) 12th

QUESTION 130: How many doubles did HOFer Harry Heilmann hit in his first season with the Reds? It was also Heilmann's last full season with the team.

a) 37
b) 28
c) 43
d) 49

TOP OF THE SEVENTH ANSWER KEY

___ **QUESTION 121:** A – 3
___ **QUESTION 122:** D – Joey Votto
___ **QUESTION 123:** B – 3
___ **QUESTION 124:** B – 100
___ **QUESTION 125:** B – 31
___ **QUESTION 126:** C – 33
___ **QUESTION 127:** A – Aaron Harang
___ **QUESTION 128:** C – 33
___ **QUESTION 129:** D – 12th
___ **QUESTION 130:** C – 43

KEEP A RUNNING TALLY OF YOUR CORRECT ANSWERS!

Number correct: __ / 10

Overall correct: __ / 130

BOTTOM OF THE SEVENTH

QUESTION 131: What was Travis Wood's team leading WHIP during his 2010 rookie season?
  a) 1.51
  b) 1.20
  c) 1.34
  d) 1.08

QUESTION 132: Jeff Shaw had a 2.38 ERA in 1997 when he led the Reds in saves. How many saves did this star closer have that season? Through 2010 his total remains the second highest in franchise history.
  a) 37
  b) 42
  c) 51
  d) 33

QUESTION 133: In 1915 a 37-year-old outfielder named Tommy Leach was second on the club in steals. It was his only season with the Reds, but it was his tenth season with at least this number of steals ... what was his total from 1915?
  a) 20
  b) 30
  c) 40
  d) 50

QUESTION 134: How many homers did ace Fred Toney give up in 1915? It was his first year in Cincinnati.
  a) 1
  b) 7
  c) 17
  d) 27

QUESTION 135: Complete games are a rarity in today's game but it hasn't always been that way. In 1945 how many pitchers tallied at least ten complete games for the Reds?

a) 0
b) 2
c) 4
d) 6

QUESTION 136: Vada Pinson terrorized opposing pitchers during his playing days. In 1961, he led the league with 37 doubles. What place was this 22-year-old centerfielder in MVP voting that season?
a) Seventh
b) Second
c) Third
d) Tenth

QUESTION 137: Eric Davis spent his best seasons with the Reds—including every season in which he hit the century mark in RBIs. How many times did Davis surpass 100 RBIs in a season?
a) One
b) Two
c) Four
d) Six

QUESTION 138: In 2004, Danny Graves was sixth in the league in saves ... but his total was also the third highest in franchise history. How many games did he save that season?
a) 28
b) 34
c) 37
d) 41

QUESTION 139: Unless you're really old school this one's going to be tough ... but in 1923, which pitcher won 27 games with a 1.93 ERA, tossed six shutouts and completed 28 games, and labored through 322 innings?
a) Eppa Rixey
b) Pete Donohue

c) Jonathan Vander Meer
d) Dolf Luque

QUESTION 140: The 1984 Reds didn't have a good year, but a coach firing brought out an interesting thing. Although Pete Rose is a strange guy, he did lead the Reds to a 19-22 record as a player-manager. It's a losing record, but it's better than the 51-70 mark by original Manager Vernon Rapp. So tell me, what was Rose's batting average in the 107 plate appearances he had as player-manager in 1984?

a) .191
b) .227
c) .275
d) .365

BOTTOM OF THE SEVENTH ANSWER KEY

___ QUESTION 131: D – 1.08
___ QUESTION 132: B – 42
___ QUESTION 133: A – 20
___ QUESTION 134: A – 1
___ QUESTION 135: C – 4
___ QUESTION 136: C – Third
___ QUESTION 137: B – Two
___ QUESTION 138: D – 41
___ QUESTION 139: D – Dolf Luque
___ QUESTION 140: D – .365

KEEP A RUNNING TALLY OF YOUR CORRECT ANSWERS!

Number correct: ___ / 10

Overall correct: ___ / 140

"When you come up to a team and see people like Joe Morgan, Johnny Bench, Tony Pérez, Pete Rose, you have to be a little awed. You ask yourself, 'what am I doing here?' But I remember what my brother Bill used to say all the time, 'Kenny, when you walk out there do your thing, remember you're as good as anybody else' and I've always felt that way."
— *Ken Griffey*

Ken Griffey

UNLIKE MANY OF the stars that made up the "Great 8"—the everyday players for the Big Red Machine—Ken Griffey, Sr. was not a top draft pick or a highly valued prospect. He was a product of the Reds farm system, but he wasn't selected until the 29th round of the 1969 draft. Nonetheless, he debuted for the club in August 1973, and by 1975 he was the starting right fielder.

That season he batted .305 with a .391 on-base percentage, setting the table quite nicely from the top of the order for the powerful hitters that followed—he scored 95 runs in only 132 games. It was the first of five seasons in which Griffey hit .300 or better. Like the other big names who made up these great 1970s clubs, Griffey came back the next season and produced again, proving he was a fixture in the lineup by scoring 111 runs in 1976 and 117 runs in 1977.

He nearly won the 1976 batting title as well, dueling it out with Chicago's Bill Madlock until the season's final day before coming up just short. Griffey batted a career high .336, and he also established career highs in on-base percentage (.401), steals (34), hits (189), and earned the first of three All-Star selections.

Any pain he felt from losing the race for the batting title was forgotten when the Reds won their second consecutive World Series title, sweeping the Yankees in four games. And while it's true that Griffey struggled in that series (he was just 1 for 17 at the plate), it's also true that he'd had a great NLCS vs. Philly (5 for 13) in a three-game sweep. And it's not like Griffey didn't have any great postseason moments, either. It's much easier to remember the World Series heroics of Tony Pérez, Pete Rose, and Joe Morgan than it is to recall who set the table for Rose during Game 7 of the 1975 World Series vs. Boston. The Red Sox led 3-2 in the seventh when Griffey drew a free pass. Not nearly as memorable as the home run Pérez hit against Bill

Lee that made it a 3-2 ballgame, not nearly as memorable as the hit Rose got to tie the game, and for sure not as memorable as the hit Morgan got to win it in the ninth, but ... it's a shame people forget Griffey stole second base with two outs to get into scoring position. It is true that Ed Armbrister later walked prior to the game-tying hit by Rose—which would have moved Griffey into scoring position anyway—but that doesn't change the fact Griffey delivered in the clutch on the base paths against a formidable opponent (Carlton Fisk) on the biggest stage of them all: World Series, Game 7.

Griffey left the club after 1981, but after six seasons with the Yankees and Braves he returned to Cincinnati during the 1988 season.

In his second tour of duty he was no longer the young speedster trying to prove he belonged—now he was the veteran ballplayer who the younger generation looked up to and sought to learn from. Griffey played that role perfectly through mid-1990, but in the midst of a season in which the team was in first every single day, he was a casualty of roster moves that August and was released to free up space. The 1990 club, of course, went on to win the World Series. Griffey missed out on playing in that series, but the team still awarded him a full World Series share for his contributions that season—and with his service that season, Griffey played for his third different Reds team to win the World Series, something no one else in franchise history has ever done.

As disappointing as his 1990 release was, Griffey was able to achieve something else that was truly extraordinary that year. He signed with the Seattle Mariners and got to play big league baseball with his son, Ken Griffey, Jr.—and on September 14, the father-son duo homered in the same game, something that had never been done before in baseball history.

Griffey's final honor as a baseball player came in 2004, when he was elected to the Reds Hall of Fame.

TOP OF THE EIGHTH

QUESTION 141: In 1984, John Franco wasn't yet a legendary closer. However, he showed good use in the pen working for closer Ted Power. What was Franco's team leading ERA during this year among all pitchers with at least 50 innings pitched?
- a) 2.61
- b) 1.77
- c) 3.00
- d) 2.00

QUESTION 142: The 1963 Reds hit just 122 home runs—the sixth lowest total out of ten teams in the league. In the past, the Reds pitching staff has been known to contribute to the club's home run total putting some guys out there who swing a pretty powerful bat ... but was that the case in 1963? How many of the club's 122 home runs were hit by a member of the Reds pitching staff that season?
- a) 0
- b) 3
- c) 7
- d) 11

QUESTION 143: The 1963 Reds did see some pretty spectacular feats from its pitching staff. The three J's—Jim Maloney, Jim O'Toole, and Joe Nuxhall—accomplished all but which one of the following stats that season?
- a) Posted ERAs below 3.00
- b) Pitched at least 200 innings
- c) Recorded at least 200 strikeouts
- d) Won at least 15 games

QUESTION 144: In 1953, Fred Baczewski was listed as the team's fifth starter in the five-man rotation. However, he led the team in three statistics. Which one of these stats did he *not* lead the team in?

a) Games started
b) WHIP
c) Complete games
d) Winning percentage

QUESTION 145: In the tumultuous 2003 season how many different skippers took the helm for at least one game with the Reds?
a) 1
b) 2
c) 3
d) 4

QUESTION 146: According to WAR, what year was the best of Aaron Boone's career with the Reds?
a) 1998
b) 1999
c) 2002
d) 2003

QUESTION 147: In 1926 the Reds were first in the league with 120 triples ... but second to last with just 35 home runs. Edd Roush led the club with seven long balls. How many players hit more homers than triples for the Reds that year?
a) 0
b) 1
c) 2
d) 3

QUESTION 148: Saves weren't an official statistic in 1911, but if they had been then Harry Gasper would have been the team leader with ... four. Gasper also led the team in another category with 17 ... what?
a) Wins
b) Complete games
c) Losses
d) Shutouts

QUESTION **149:** Which of the following was the Reds' first stadium?
- a) Great American Ballpark
- b) Crosley Field
- c) Union Grounds
- d) Riverfront Stadium

QUESTION **150:** Which of the following players was the first to win a league MVP Award with the Reds?
- a) George Crowe
- b) Ernie Lombardi
- c) Johnny Bench
- d) George Foster

TOP OF THE EIGHTH ANSWER KEY

___ **QUESTION 141:** A – 2.61
___ **QUESTION 142:** A – 0
___ **QUESTION 143:** C – Recorded at least 200 strikeouts
___ **QUESTION 144:** A – Games started
___ **QUESTION 145:** C – 3
___ **QUESTION 146:** C – 2002
___ **QUESTION 147:** B – 1
___ **QUESTION 148:** C – Losses
___ **QUESTION 149:** C – Union Grounds
___ **QUESTION 150:** B – Ernie Lombardi

KEEP A RUNNING TALLY OF YOUR CORRECT ANSWERS!

Number correct: ___ / 10

Overall correct: ___ / 150

BOTTOM OF THE EIGHTH

QUESTION 151: Tom Browning was a 20-game winner as a rookie in 1985 ... yet he didn't win Rookie of the Year honors. Who beat out Browning as the top rookie in the N.L.?
a) Doc Gooden
b) John Tudor
c) Vince Coleman
d) Darryl Strawberry

QUESTION 152: Who pitched the first perfect game in franchise history?
a) Tom Seaver
b) Johnny Vander Meer
c) Tom Browning
d) Mario Soto

QUESTION 153: Which pitcher won the most games for the Reds during the 1990s?
a) Mario Soto
b) Jose Rijo
c) Tom Browning
d) John Smiley

QUESTION 154: Which player had the most steals for the Reds during the 1990s?
a) Barry Larkin
b) Chris Sabo
c) Eric Davis
d) Reggie Sanders

QUESTION 155: In 1978 Tom Seaver was the only member of the Reds pitching staff to toe the rubber for more than 200 innings—and he did so with a team-best 2.88 ERA. What other notable stat did he achieve that season to lead the team?
a) Five shutouts
b) 200 strikeouts

c) 11 complete games
d) Two no-hitters

QUESTION 156: Also in 1978, Doug Bair posted an incredible 1.97 ERA out of the bullpen and was third in the league with a career high in saves. How many games did the Reds closer save that season?
a) 25
b) 28
c) 31
d) 34

QUESTION 157: In 1964 the pitching staff carried the club and nearly won a Pennant. The Reds placed second in the league and the staff posted a team 3.07 ERA that was also second best in the league. With nine guys who totaled more than 50 innings on the mound ... how many of them posted an ERA under 3.50?
a) 3
b) 5
c) 7
d) 9

QUESTION 158: What was Ewell Blackwell's nickname?
a) Whipped Cream
b) Well Done
c) The Whip
d) Noodle

QUESTION 159: In 1947, Ewell Blackwell led the league in wins, complete games, strikeouts per nine innings, and strikeouts to walk ratio ... but where did he finish in the MVP race?
a) 1st
b) 2nd
c) 4th
d) 7th

QUESTION 160: Greg Vaughn led the club in homers in 1999, but despite his prodigious total he was only third in the league. How many home runs did Vaughn hit that year?
- a) 43
- b) 45
- c) 47
- d) 49

BOTTOM OF THE EIGHTH ANSWER KEY

___ **QUESTION 151:** C – Vince Coleman
___ **QUESTION 152:** C – Tom Browning
___ **QUESTION 153:** B – Jose Rijo
___ **QUESTION 154:** A – Barry Larkin
___ **QUESTION 155:** B – 200 strikeouts
___ **QUESTION 156:** B – 28
___ **QUESTION 157:** C – 7
___ **QUESTION 158:** C – The Whip
___ **QUESTION 159:** B – 2nd
___ **QUESTION 160:** B – 45

KEEP A RUNNING TALLY OF YOUR CORRECT ANSWERS!

Number correct: ___ / 10

Overall correct: ___ / 160

"My dream as a boy always had been to play alongside Mickey Mantle. The Yankees as a team were my heroes. But at this minute, I would not want to trade uniforms."
— César Gerónimo, after sweeping the Yankees in the 1976 World Series

César Gerónimo

HE'S THE ANSWER to one of the best baseball trivia questions of all-time: who was the 3,000th career strikeout victim for both Nolan Ryan *and* Bob Gibson? And while most of us mortals who never got the chance to play big league baseball wouldn't mind at all being an historical footnote next to the names of Hall of Fame legends like Ryan and Gibson, it's much less fun for a professional athlete to be a mere footnote. Well, in this case there's no need to worry about César Gerónimo ... his career numbers, accomplishments, and the accolades he's received from his peers and coaches speak far louder than a couple of asterisks.

He is, after all, a member of the Reds Hall of Fame—and for good reason.

Gerónimo was part of the trade that brought Joe Morgan to the club, having spent his first three seasons in the majors playing for the Houston Astros. With the Astros he was only a part-time player, used in late innings for defensive purposes or on the bases as a pinch-runner—but in 1972, his first season with the Reds, he batted .275 in 285 plate appearances. He'd batted just .228 in 138 plate appearances during three seasons with the Astros.

His improvement at the plate was huge in terms of his contribution to the club's success, because his defense was just too good for him to play only part-time. Reds hitting coach Ted Kluszewski said about his defense, "Not only is his arm incredibly strong, it's also accurate. No one, I mean no one, runs on him." Kluszewski's praise wasn't just hyperbole, either. Gerónimo's arm was so good that the Reds considered converting him to a pitcher, despite the fact he'd already spent three years in the majors as an outfielder. It was his bat that had relegated him to part-time status, but 1972 was the turning point in his career—and with some success at the plate, he became the Reds everyday centerfielder.

He won four consecutive Gold Gloves from 1974-77, but the defensive genius was also a star at the plate during both the 1975 and 1976 World Series'.

After being maligned for his lack of offense for much of his career, Gerónimo batted .280 with two home runs, a triple, three runs, and three RBIs vs. Boston during the 1975 World Series, and then he batted .308 with two doubles, two steals, and three runs vs. New York during the 1976 World Series. The man who's defense Sparky Anderson called "ungodly" became an offensive star on baseball's biggest stage.

And so what if he struck out against Nolan Ryan and Bob Gibson at a rather inopportune time ... he's also a two-time world champion who was elected to the Reds Hall of Fame in 2008.

TOP OF THE NINTH

QUESTION 161: According to WAR, who was the best player for the star-studded 1999 Cincinnati Reds—Mike Cameron or Greg Vaughn?

QUESTION 162: In 2008, who was the Reds leading pitcher with a record of 17-6?

QUESTION 163: Also in 2008, who was the Reds leader in a less glamorous category ... losses? In fact, his record was the exact opposite of the pitcher who led the team in wins: 6-17.

QUESTION 164: The 1919 Reds were the first in franchise history to appear in a modern-era World Series and the club made the most of the opportunity, beating the Chicago White Sox in the series. The White Sox won three games during the 1919 World Series. How many games did the Reds win?

QUESTION 165: Who led the Reds with four shutouts in 1948—Johnny Vander Meer or Ken Raffensberger?

QUESTION 166: In 1995 which was the higher total—Jeff Brantley's saves or Pete Schourek and John Smiley's combined wins?

QUESTION 167: How many times did Hall of Fame legend Frank Robinson get 200-plus hits in a season during his career with the Reds?

QUESTION 168: Who led the 1969 Reds with 38 home runs— Lee May or Tony Pérez?

QUESTION 169: Who led the 1969 Reds with 122 RBIs—Lee May or Tony Pérez?

QUESTION 170: True or False: A player named Snake Deal once played for the Cincinnati Reds.

TOP OF THE NINTH ANSWER KEY

___ **QUESTION 161:** Mike Cameron
___ **QUESTION 162:** Edinson Volquez
___ **QUESTION 163:** Aaron Harang
___ **QUESTION 164:** Five
___ **QUESTION 165:** Ken Raffensberger
___ **QUESTION 166:** Schourek and Smiley, 30 wins – Brantley 28
          saves
___ **QUESTION 167:** One, 1962
___ **QUESTION 168:** Lee May
___ **QUESTION 169:** Tony Pérez
___ **QUESTION 170:** True – although his given name was John
          Wesley ...

KEEP A RUNNING TALLY OF YOUR CORRECT ANSWERS!

Number correct: __ / 10

Overall correct: __ / 170

BOTTOM OF THE NINTH

QUESTION 171: In which season did the Reds win a franchise record 108 games—1970 or 1975?

QUESTION 172: How many times have the Reds won the World Series by sweeping the opposing team—never or two?

QUESTION 173: In which season did the Reds score a franchise record 865 runs—1976 or 1999?

QUESTION 174: In which season did the Reds set a franchise record with a .296 team batting average—1922 or 2010?

QUESTION 175: In which season did the Reds set a franchise record by belting 222 home runs—1990 or 2005?

QUESTION 176: What is the franchise record for most consecutive games with at least one home run (team)—21 or 23?

QUESTION 177: In which season did the Reds set a franchise record by smashing nine grand slams—2002 or 2005?

QUESTION 178: In which season did the Reds set a franchise record by accumulating a staggering 572 extra-base hits—2002 or 2005?

QUESTION 179: What is the franchise record for most stolen bases (team) in a season—230 or 310?

QUESTION 180: Who set a franchise record after batting .377 in a single season—Lee May or Cy Seymour?

Bottom of the Ninth Answer Key

___ **Question 171:** 1975
___ **Question 172:** Two, 1976 and 1990
___ **Question 173:** 1999
___ **Question 174:** 1922
___ **Question 175:** 2005
___ **Question 176:** 21
___ **Question 177:** 2002
___ **Question 178:** 2005
___ **Question 179:** 310
___ **Question 180:** Cy Seymour

Keep a running tally of your correct answers!

Number correct: ___ / 10

Overall correct: ___ / 180

"Gary Nolan is the most complete pitcher in the National League."
— Larry Shepard, former Reds pitching coach

Gary Nolan

THE BOTTOM LINE is no matter how good your offense is, you still need pitching and defense to win championships. And with Gary Nolan, the Big Red Machine had one of the best talents of his generation on the mound.

True, his name might not strike fear into the hearts of all you free-swinging power hitters out there—at least not in the same way as, say, Tom Seaver ... but without question he was one of the most talented pitchers in baseball during the Big Red Machine era, and except for countless injuries that plagued him year after year he'd have the numbers and awards to back up that claim.

Consider the history of Nolan—he was the Reds first-round draft choice (#13 overall) in 1966 as an 18-year-old kid straight out of high school. He spent the rest of 1966 pitching for Class A Sioux Falls—but on April 15, 1967, less than a year after he was drafted, and still only 18 years old, he made his big league debut and pitched seven innings in a 7-3 victory vs. the Houston Astros. He didn't turn 19 for another two months, but by then he was 3-1 on the season with 60 strikeouts in only 57 innings and a miniscule 2.37 earned run average. He'd also thrown two complete games, one of them a shutout. By season's end he'd compiled a 14-8 record that included eight complete games, *five* shutouts, and 206 strikeouts—and all of those numbers were the best in major league history for any pitcher who started a season only 18 years old or younger.

He even struck out Willie Mays four times ... *in the same game!*

Was he Rookie of the Year?

No ... only placed third. You might recall this was 1967 and another rookie phenom was on the mound for the Mets ... a guy named Tom Seaver.

Nolan's career might have gone the same route as Seaver's if not for the injuries that began plaguing him his sophomore season. He strained his shoulder in Spring Training, 1968. He still returned later in the year and posted a terrific 9-4 record. He was the Opening Day starter for the Reds in 1969, and he fanned 12 Dodgers in a 3-2 loss—but in his very next start he pulled a muscle and was sidelined for three months. He won 18 games to help the Reds win the N.L. West in 1970.

It was his fourth big league season and he was still only 22 years old. So how'd he do in the postseason?

He helped the Reds win the N.L. Pennant over Pittsburgh, of course. In Game 1 of the best-of-five series he scattered eight hits over nine shutout innings. The game was scoreless after nine, but the Reds pushed three runs across in the top of the tenth and Nolan got the victory, 3-0, after Clay Carroll pitched a scoreless frame in the bottom of the tenth.

In 1972, he was a staggering 13-2 with a 1.82 earned run average ... *at the All-Star break.*

When he was healthy, Nolan was one of the game's best—the problem, of course, is he was injury prone his entire career. He pitched only two games in 1973 and missed all of 1974 after suffering from bone spurs in his shoulder.

With the "Great 8" assembled and ready to win in 1975, the burden of finishing the postseason with a victory rested squarely on the shoulders of Nolan and the rest of the pitching staff. And for the Big Red Machine teams of 1975-76, Nolan was up to the task.

He was 15-9 in 1975, and 15-9 again in 1976.

You can find his name all over the leader boards for those two seasons—but what that really means, and why that is really important, is that every time he took the mound the Reds had a chance to win.

And the biggest win of his career?

Only 28 years old but in his ninth big league season, he started and won Game 4 of the 1976 World Series. That victory gave the Reds a second consecutive title and assured the team's place in history as a dynasty. Less than a year later his career was over, the injuries too significant to make another comeback and far too frequent to make him a household name for many of today's fans—but for the Big Red Machine, his name was just as vital as Bench or Rose or Morgan.

TOP OF THE TENTH

QUESTION 181: Who set a franchise record after belting 52 home runs in a single season—Frank Robinson or George Foster?

QUESTION 182: Who set a franchise record after he scored 134 runs in a single season—Frank Robinson or Eric Davis?

QUESTION 183: Who was the first player in franchise history to belt three grand slams in a single season—Lee May or Frank Robinson?

QUESTION 184: Which player hit a franchise record 34 home runs at home during a single season—Ted Kluszewski or Frank Robinson?

QUESTION 185: Which player hit a franchise record 31 home runs on the road during a single season—Ken Griffey, Jr. or George Foster?

QUESTION 186: In August 1962, Frank Robinson set a franchise record when he hit 14 home runs in a single month. That record was tied in September 1999 by which player—Mike Cameron or Greg Vaughn?

QUESTION 187: Who was the first player in franchise history to hit two home runs in the same inning—Pete Rose or Ray Knight?

QUESTION 188: Which player set a franchise record with 149 RBIs in a single season—Frank Robinson or George Foster?

QUESTION **189**: Which pitcher set a modern era (post-1900) franchise record with 27 wins in 1923—Eppa Rixey or Dolf Luque?

QUESTION **190**: Which pitcher set a franchise record with 16 consecutive wins—Ewell Blackwell or Tom Seaver?

TOP OF THE TENTH ANSWER KEY

___ **QUESTION 181:** George Foster
___ **QUESTION 182:** Frank Robinson
___ **QUESTION 183:** Frank Robinson
___ **QUESTION 184:** Ted Kluszewski
___ **QUESTION 185:** George Foster
___ **QUESTION 186:** Greg Vaughn
___ **QUESTION 187:** Ray Knight
___ **QUESTION 188:** George Foster
___ **QUESTION 189:** Dolf Luque
___ **QUESTION 190:** Ewell Blackwell

KEEP A RUNNING TALLY OF YOUR CORRECT ANSWERS!

Number correct: ___ / 10

Overall correct: ___ / 190

Bottom of the Tenth

Question 191: Who won more career games for the Reds—Jack Billingham or Tom Seaver?

Question 192: Who won more career games for the Reds—Mario Soto or Jose Rijo?

Question 193: Who is the all-time franchise leader in career saves with 182—John Franco or Danny Graves?

Question 194: Will White pitched a franchise record eight shutouts for the Reds in 1882. The modern era record for shutouts in a season is seven. Who was the most recent player to record seven shutouts in a single season—Jose Rijo or Jack Billingham?

Question 195: Who pitched more career shutouts for the Reds—Mario Soto or Tom Browning?

Question 196: Who once batted .348 for one of the top-ten season averages in franchise history—Pete Rose or Barry Larkin?

Question 197: Who posted a higher career batting average for the Reds—Barry Larkin or Joe Morgan?

Question 198: Who holds both the season and career franchise records for on-base percentage—Joe Morgan or Frank Robinson?

Question 199: Who holds the franchise record with a career .554 slugging percentage—Adam Dunn or Frank Robinson?

Question 200: Dave Parker and Austin Kearns both rank among the top 25 in franchise history for career slugging percentage ... but which one ranks higher—Dave Parker or Austin Kearns?

Bottom of the Tenth Answer Key

___ **Question 191:** Jack Billingham 87, Tom Seaver 75
___ **Question 192:** Mario Soto 100, Jose Rijo 97
___ **Question 193:** Danny Graves
___ **Question 194:** Jack Billingham, 1973
___ **Question 195:** Mario Soto 13, Tom Browning 12
___ **Question 196:** Pete Rose, 1969
___ **Question 197:** Barry Larkin .295, Joe Morgan .288
___ **Question 198:** Joe Morgan .466, 1975; .415, career
___ **Question 199:** Frank Robinson
___ **Question 200:** Dave Parker .469, Austin Kearns .468

Keep a running tally of your correct answers!

Number correct: ___ / 10

Overall correct: ___ / 200

Cincinnati Reds IQ

It's time to find out your Reds IQ. Add your total from all ten chapters and see how you did! Here's how it breaks down:

GENIUS REDS IQ EXCEEDS SPARKY ANDERSON	= 190-200
GENIUS REDS IQ DESTINED TO BE A FIRST BALLOT HALL OF FAMER	= 180-189
GENIUS REDS IQ IS WORTHY OF A WORLD CHAMPIONSHIP	= 170-179
SUPERIOR REDS IQ IS WORTHY OF LEGENDARY STATUS	= 160-169
SUPERIOR REDS IQ MAKES YOU ONE OF THE ALL-TIME GREATS	= 150-159
OUTSTANDING REDS IQ THAT PLACES YOU AMONG THE TOP PLAYERS	= 140-149
ABOVE AVERAGE REDS IQ THAT EARNS YOU A NICE PAYCHECK	= 130-139
SOLID REDS IQ THAT LETS YOU PLAY BALL FOR A LIVING	= 120-129
AVERAGE REDS IQ GOOD ENOUGH TO GET YOU TO THE SHOW	= 110-119
AVERAGE REDS IQ GOT YOU A CUP OF COFFEE BUT THAT'S ALL	= 100-109

How'd you do? I'd like to know. Send me an email: tckrelliot@gmail.com

Be sure to tell me how many questions you got right, and if you scored high enough, you might just make your way onto a Hall of Fame list to be included in Volume II of Cincinnati Reds IQ.

If you enjoyed reading this book, please consider posting a review online at Amazon.com or wherever you buy books—and don't be shy about posting your Reds IQ, either.

About the Authors

TUCKER ELLIOT is a Georgia native and a diehard baseball fan. A former high school athletic director and varsity baseball coach, he now writes fulltime. He has authored or contributed to more than two-dozen books on baseball history and trivia.

JOE SORIANO is a prolific sports blogger and you can find him pontificating daily on everything sports-related at prosportswrap.com. He's also the author of a soon-to-be-published book on underrated football players.

References

WEBSITES
Baseball-reference.com
MLB.com (and the official team sites through MLB.com)
BaseballHallofFame.org
ESPN.com

BOOKS
Baseball, an Illustrated History, Geoffrey C. Ward and Ken
        Burns
The Team by Team Encyclopedia of Major League Baseball,
        Dennis Purdy
The Unofficial Guide to Baseball's Most Unusual Records, Bob
        Mackin
The 2005 ESPN Baseball Encyclopedia, edited by Pete Palmer
        and Gary Gillette
100 Years of the World Series, Eric Enders

About Black Mesa

BLACK MESA IS a Florida-based publishing company that specializes in sports history and trivia books. Look for these popular titles in our trivia IQ series:

- *Mixed Martial Arts (Volumes I & II)*
- *Boston Red Sox (Volumes I & II)*
- *Tampa Bay Rays*
- *New York Yankees*
- *Atlanta Braves*
- *Milwaukee Brewers*
- *St. Louis Cardinals (Volumes I & II)*
- *Major League Baseball*
- *Boston Celtics*
- *Florida Gators Football*
- *Georgia Bulldogs Football*
- *Texas Longhorns Football*
- *Oklahoma Sooners Football*
- *Texas A&M Aggies Football*
- *New England Patriots*

For information about special discounts for bulk purchases, please email:

black.mesa.publishing@gmail.com

www.blackmesabooks.com

Also in the Sports by the Numbers Series

- *Major League Baseball*
- *New York Yankees*
- *Boston Red Sox*
- *San Francisco Giants*
- *Texas Rangers*
- *University of Oklahoma Football*
- *University of Georgia Football*
- *Penn State University Football*
- *NASCAR*
- *Sacramento Kings Basketball*
- *Mixed Martial Arts*

The following is an excerpt from

Major League Baseball IQ: The Ultimate Test of True Fandom

Tucker Elliot

2010 Edition (Volume I)

Available from Black Mesa Publishing

First

THERE'S A REASON DIEHARD FANS GET TO THE BALLPARK hours before game time. It's not for better parking. It's not for extra time to find our seats. It's not so we'll have time to down an extra hot dog, heavy on the mustard, prior to the first pitch.

It's called BP.

Watching a Major League team take batting practice is without question one of the most exhilarating events a baseball fan can witness firsthand. But we don't go hours early to watch players practice hitting to the opposite field. Oh no, we want to see the long ball, and lots of them. That's why we bring our gloves. It's partly because we want to chase those big flies and try to catch one like we're little kids ... and partly because we know if Albert Pujols drills one right at us that having a glove is truly a matter of life or death.

There isn't a fan alive that doesn't love the long ball.

So that's where we begin. Here in the top of the first we've got a heavy dose of big-time sluggers who performed some incredible feats. Let's get going with those two immortal words we love so much: *Play Ball!*

TOP OF THE FIRST

QUESTION 1: The annual Home Run Derby during the All-Star break has been a fan-favorite for a long time. The All-Star break has also been a historical measuring stick for players on a potential record-setting home run pace. If you've got 30 bombs at the break, well, that's pretty special. Who was the first player in history to hit 30 home runs before the All-Star break?
   a) Dave Kingman
   b) Willie Mays
   c) Harmon Killebrew
   d) Mike Schmidt

QUESTION 2: The list of players to hit 30 homers before the break is pretty short, but it's also pretty stout because it's a virtual who's who of home run champions. A few guys have done it more than once, but only one player has made it to the break with 30 homers on four different occasions. Who is that player?

a) Ken Griffey, Jr.
b) Sammy Sosa
c) Mark McGwire
d) Alex Rodriguez

QUESTION 3: In 1994, for the first time in history, there were three players who hit 30 homers prior to the All-Star break. In 1998, that record was eclipsed as four players went into the break with at least 30 homers. In both seasons—1994 and 1998—there was one slugger who was a part of both of those record-setting groups. Who had at least 30 homers at the All-Star break in both 1994 and 1998?
a) Greg Vaughn
b) Mark McGwire
c) Ken Griffey, Jr.
d) Sammy Sosa

QUESTION 4: Who is the only slugger in history to make it to the All-Star break with at least 30 homers ... for two different teams?
a) Ken Griffey, Jr.
b) Mark McGwire
c) Reggie Jackson
d) Greg Vaughn

QUESTION 5: Only five players in history have made it to the All-Star break with at least 35 home runs. The record is 39. Who holds that record?
a) Mark McGwire
b) Luis Gonzalez
c) Ken Griffey, Jr.
d) Barry Bonds

QUESTION 6: Who was the first player in history to make it to the All-Star break with at least 30 homers and *not* win his league's home run title?
a) Reggie Jackson
b) Greg Vaughn
c) Willie Mays
d) Dave Kingman

QUESTION 7: Frank Thomas—not the Big Hurt, but the original Frank Thomas who debuted for the Pittsburgh Pirates on August 17, 1951, and finished his initial rookie campaign with two home runs—slugged 30 homers in 1953, his first full big league season, and was an All-Star the following year. He later set a Major League record for a particular type of home run—that being the clutch walk-off game-winning variety. Thomas was the first player in big league history to win a game for each of four different franchises via a walk-off home run: the Pirates, Braves, Mets, and Phillies. Over the years several others players have tied his record, most recently a high-profile free agent signee in his first year with his new club in 2010. His game-winning shot came vs. Scot Shields of the LA Angels. Who tied the Major League record by hitting a walk-off blast for his fourth ballclub on May 1, 2010?

   a)   Johnny Damon
   b)   Alfonso Soriano
   c)   Andruw Jones
   d)   Troy Glaus

QUESTION 8: And staying with that particular home run record ... prior to 2010, it was a member of the Tampa Bay Rays who tied this record by drilling a walk-off blast for his fourth different team. Who tied this record as a member of the Rays?

   a)   Vinny Castilla
   b)   Jose Canseco
   c)   Carlos Pena
   d)   Fred McGriff

QUESTION 9: On May 1, 2010, a member of the Arizona Diamondbacks doubled and singled in his first two at bats vs. the Cubs to raise his season average to .667. Okay, he was only 9 for 12 on the season ... but, he did start the season *9 for 12*, and even better the player who got off to such a hot start at the plate in 2010 was Dan Haren, who doesn't earn the big paycheck to swing the bat, but rather to make other guys who also earn big paychecks look flat-out stupid trying to make contact with Uncle Charlie. In nearly 40 years of baseball since the DH rule was instituted in the AL only one other pitcher had a better stretch of at bats than Haren's run to begin 2010. A member of the 2001 San Francisco Giants pitching staff had a stretch in which he was 12 for 13. Now that's just ridiculous. Which member of the 2001 Giants pitching staff apparently thought he was Barry Bonds for a spell?

a) Jason Schmidt
b) Kirk Rueter
c) Russ Ortiz
d) Livan Hernandez

QUESTION 10: The Los Angeles Dodgers are steeped in history and tradition, recognized around the world as one of the premiere franchises in professional sports, not just MLB. So to have your name etched in the Dodgers' franchise record book for something no one else has ever done is quite special to say the least. This is the franchise, after all, of Reese, Lasorda, Snider, Koufax, Campanella, Robinson, Drysdale, and ... Don Demeter? Yup, Demeter, who hit only 34 home runs in five seasons for the Dodgers, set a franchise record in 1959 that stood half a century. It was a hot start at the plate that got Demeter's name in the book after he belted five homers with 14 RBI and a .382 batting average during the first nine home games on the Dodgers' schedule that season. No other Dodgers' player had ever posted such gaudy numbers in the three Triple Crown categories during the club's first nine home games ... and no player did so again, not until 2010 that is, when this player batted *.432* with five home runs and 14 RBI during the Dodgers first nine home games. Who set the new standard for hot starts at home for the Dodgers franchise?

a) Matt Kemp
b) Manny Ramirez
c) Andre Ethier
d) James Loney

TOP OF THE FIRST ANSWER KEY

___ **QUESTION 1:** B
___ **QUESTION 2:** C
___ **QUESTION 3:** C
___ **QUESTION 4:** B
___ **QUESTION 5:** D
___ **QUESTION 6:** C
___ **QUESTION 7:** A*
___ **QUESTION 8:** C*
___ **QUESTION 9:** D*
___ **QUESTION 10:** C

KEEP A RUNNING TALLY OF YOUR CORRECT ANSWERS!

Number correct: ___ / 10

Overall correct: ___ / 10

#7 – Royals, Red Sox, Yankees, and Tigers.
#8 – Athletics, Tigers, Red Sox, and Rays.
#9 – He was 15 for 64 on the season: .296, one home run, eight RBI, and only four strikeouts.

Bottom of the First

QUESTION 11: The National League began play in 1876, thus the player who led the league in home runs that season was, for a brief time, baseball's all-time leading home run hitter. His name was George Hall and he played in Philadelphia. And as the baseball gods often orchestrate, the stars were aligned just so and the result is this obscure yet fascinating bit of trivia: on July 15, 1876, when Hall homered for the final time that season (therefore, setting the first-ever season home run record) on that same day George Bradley, pitching for St. Louis, tossed the first-ever no-hitter in big league history. Bradley won 45 games that season and enjoyed a much longer and more successful career than did Hall, who the following season was homerless and later banned from baseball for fixing games. Still, he was baseball's first home run champ. How many home runs did it take for George Hall to establish the first season home run record in 1876?

    a) 3
    b) 5
    c) 7
    d) 9

QUESTION 12: George Hall's home run record lasted three years. Boston's Charley Jones broke it in 1879, and unlike Hall, Jones continued to produce and enjoy big league success, setting another record the following season when he became the first player in history to hit two home runs in the same inning. How many home runs did Charley Jones hit in 1879 to establish a new big league record?

    a) 5
    b) 7
    c) 9
    d) 11

QUESTION 13: Harry Stovey tied for the league lead with six home runs in 1880, and then in 1883 the five-time home run champion broke the season record previously set by Charley Jones when he hit 14 four-baggers. That same season, Cincinnati, in the American Association, established a professional record by belting 35 home runs ... as a team! Well, both the individual and team records didn't last long. That's because in 1884 Chicago and Ned Williamson went on a power binge. Williamson shattered the home run record with *27* (and became the first player to hit three homers in a single game) and his club belted *142 long balls.* The top four home run hitters in the league all played for Chicago! And the reason for this power surge was ...

    a)   Rampant HGH usage

    b)   Corked bats

    c)   Greg Anderson's (Barry Bonds' trainer) great-great-great-grandfather was Chicago's trainer that year

    d)   Lakefront Park dimensions (where Chicago played its home games): 196 feet to right, 252 to right-center, 300 to left-center, and 180 down the left field line

QUESTION 14: Ned Williamson's home run record stood for 35 years. Babe Ruth, who led the league with 11 home runs in 1918, blasted 29 home runs in 1919 to establish a new record. The record-breaking blast came in the ninth with his team trailing 1-0. It tied the score, sent the game to extra-innings, and Ruth's club won it in the 13th inning. Against which team did Babe Ruth break the single-season home run record for the first time in his career?

    a)   Boston Red Sox

    b)   New York Yankees

    c)   Detroit Tigers

    d)   St. Louis Browns

QUESTION 15: The year Ruth hit 60 home runs, in 1927, he and Lou Gehrig established a Major League record for teammates, combining for 107 home runs. That record fell on September 9, 1961, when Roger Maris homered vs. Cleveland for his 56th long ball of the season—and combined with the 52 Mickey Mantle had at the time, gave the powerful duo 108 on the season. Maris, of course, went on to break Ruth's single-season record when he went yard on October 1—the season's final day—for his 61st home run. Against which team did Maris homer to break Ruth's single-season home run record?

    a)   Boston Red Sox

    b)   Detroit Tigers

    c)   Chicago White Sox

    d)   Cleveland Indians

QUESTION 16: A big home run is a definite game-changer—and a pinch-hit home run, well, that's really special. What about a guy who consistently belts pinch-hit home runs? You get a guy like that on your team and good things are bound to happen. Only one player in Major League history has hit as many as four pinch-hit home runs in back-to-back seasons. Who is he?

 a) George Crowe
 b) Gates Brown
 c) Cliff Johnson
 d) Lenny Harris

QUESTION 17: How about the Major League record for most pinch-hit home runs in one season? Joe Cronin holds the A.L. record with five for the 1943 Boston Red Sox, but he was one short of the then Major League record six set by Brooklyn's Johnny Frederick in 1932. Frederick's record stood until 2000. A member of the Dodgers hit seven pinch-hit home runs in 2000 to establish a new record, and the following season, a member of the Pittsburgh Pirates tied the new record when he also hit seven pinch-hit home runs. Can you identify the two players with seven pinch-hit homers in 2000 and 2001?

 a) Devon White and Gary Matthews
 b) Todd Hollandsworth and Brian Giles
 c) Dave Hansen and Craig Wilson
 d) Jim Leyritz and John Vander Wal

QUESTION 18: Staying with the pinch-hitters ... Lenny Harris pinch-hit a N.L. record 804 times during his career and his 212 hits in that role is also a record. The leader in the A.L. is Gates Brown, who pinch-hit 414 times. The big difference? All of Brown's pinch-hit appearances came for the Detroit Tigers, but Harris ... he was a journeyman. For how many different N.L. teams did Lenny Harris get at least one pinch-hit?

 a) 6
 b) 7
 c) 8
 d) 9

QUESTION 19: The Major League record for hitting safely in consecutive pinch-hit at bats during one season is eight. Dave Philley established this record with Philadelphia in 1958. That record has never been broken, although it has been equaled. Who besides Dave Philley is the only other player in baseball history to collect eight consecutive pinch-hits?

a) Lenny Harris
b) Rusty Staub
c) Randy Bush
d) John Vander Wal

QUESTION 20: Gates Brown owns the A.L. record with 16 career pinch-hit homers. Jerry Lynch (Cincinnati and Pittsburgh) holds the N.L. record with 18 pinch-hit homers. The player who owns the Major League record isn't all that close to being the leader in either league, because he obviously spent time playing in both the N.L. and the A.L. Who hit a Major League record 20 pinch-hit home runs during his career?
a) Rich Reese
b) Ron Northey
c) Cliff Johnson
d) Rusty Staub

˙ BOTTOM OF THE FIRST ANSWER KEY

___ QUESTION 11: B
___ QUESTION 12: C
___ QUESTION 13: D*
___ QUESTION 14: B
___ QUESTION 15: A
___ QUESTION 16: A
___ QUESTION 17: C
___ QUESTION 18: C
___ QUESTION 19: B
___ QUESTION 20: C

KEEP A RUNNING TALLY OF YOUR CORRECT ANSWERS!

Number correct: ___ / 10

Overall correct: ___ / 20

#13 – Prior to 1884, ground rules mandated balls hit over the left and right field fences were deemed doubles, but in 1884 they were ruled home runs.

www.blackmesabooks.com

Made in the USA
San Bernardino, CA
02 April 2016